D0186141

Think Through History

Medieval Minds

Britain 1066–1500

General Editors:

Christine Counsell   Michael Riley

Special Consultant:

Jamie Byrom

PEARSON
Longman

Medieval Minds – Britain 1066 to 1500

Introduction

Your enquiries

Living with death in mind

William I 1066-1087   William II 1087-1100   Henry I 1100-1135   Stephen 1135-1154   Henry II 1154-1189   Richard I 1189-1199   John 1199-1216   Henry III 1216-1272

1066 Battle of Hastings
1069 Harrying of the North begins
1086 Domesday Book
1095 First Crusade

1170 Murder of Thomas Becket
1212 Childrens' Crusade
1215 Magna Carta

Struggles for power

Struggles for minds

Edward I 1272-1307　Edward II 1307-1327　Edward III 1327-1377　Richard II 1377-1399　Henry IV 1399-1413　Henry V 1413-1422　Henry VI 1422-1471　Edward IV 1461-1483

82 Edward I's Conquest of Wales　1337 Hundred Years War begins
1295 Model Parliament　1348 Black Death
1306 Rebellion of Robert Bruce
1314 Battle of Bannockburn
1400 Owain Glyn Dŵr's rebellion begins
1453 Hundred Years War ends
1381 Peasants' Revolt
1382 John Wycliffe's English bible

Introduction

A different world from ours

14th century picture of a woman having a baby

This picture shows the birth of a baby in the Middle Ages. It is a Caesarian birth. The baby could not be born naturally so the mother has been cut to get the baby out. Nowadays Caesarian births are quite common. Maybe some people in your class were born this way.

In the Middle Ages Caesarian births were very dangerous. **Medieval** people did not know how to stop bleeding and infection. The mother in this picture is dead.

In many ways medieval people were just like you. They worked, played, argued and joked. But the world they lived in was very different from yours. People did things differently. Medieval minds worked in a different way.

Think

- How was childbirth in the Middle Ages similar to childbirth today?

- How was it different?

Medieval people lived in a different way

From a 14th-century manuscript

Think

- What is happening in this picture?
- What does the picture tell you about the way medieval people lived?

Medieval people thought in a different way

From a 15th-century painting of hell

Think

- What can you see in this picture of hell?
- What does the picture tell you about what medieval people believed?

Medieval people treated each other in a different way

From a 14th-century manuscript

Think

- Describe what you can see in this picture.
- How can you tell which person was in control in this picture?

The minds of all medieval people were ruled by the fear of death. Death was all around them. Living was dangerous. Disease or violence was always near. To learn about medieval living, you need to learn about medieval dying.

It is also very difficult to find out about medieval people. The evidence is hard to find. You have to ask lots of questions. You have to dig deep...

Digging deep

①

Who can tell us most about medieval peasants?

This is the skeleton of a medieval person. It was found in the churchyard of Wharram Percy, a village in Yorkshire. Altogether, **archaeologists** dug up more than a thousand skeletons. Scientists have carefully examined the bones. They have made some interesting discoveries ...

① Many of the skeletons were those of children.

② The skeletons of the adults were about six centimetres shorter than people are today.

③ Many of the bone-joints were worn or deformed.

④ They did not have tooth decay, but their teeth were quite worn.

Think

- What might each of these discoveries tell you about the lives of medieval people at Wharram Percy?

Your enquiry

These skeletons belonged to ordinary medieval people. We call these people **peasants**. They lived in villages and spent their time growing crops and raising animals to feed their families. We can learn quite a lot about medieval peasants from their skeletons, but bones cannot answer all our questions. We need to look at other sources as well. Which sources will help us most? We need to dig deeper.

Digging up the past

This is a photograph of Wharram Percy as it looks today. As you can see, no one lives there anymore. Almost everyone left the village at the end of the Middle Ages.

Only the ruined church and a later farmhouse remain. The bumps in the ground show you where the peasants' houses and other buildings stood.

Think

- Which of the bumps might be the peasants' houses?
- What do you think the other bumps might be?

People who dig historical sites are called archaeologists. For many years archaeologists from all over the world came to Wharram Percy to find out what life was like for ordinary people in the Middle Ages. Most of the things they found were pieces of broken pottery or animal bones, but they also found more unusual objects. Historians call these objects **artefacts**. You can see some artefacts from Wharram Percy on this page.

Think

- What do you think each of these artefacts was made from?

- What do you think medieval people used each of the artefacts for?

- What does each of the artefacts tell you about the lives of medieval peasants?

Reconstruction of the inside of peasant's house

Of course, the archaeologists did not have the time or money to dig all the peasant houses. Instead they chose to study one or two houses very carefully. On the right is a picture of an artist's **reconstruction** of what one house might have looked like.

Think

- What things in the reconstruction could not be worked out from archaeological evidence?

- What can the reconstruction tell you about the lives of medieval peasants?

This is another reconstruction. It shows what the whole village of Wharram Percy might have looked like. The group of buildings at the bottom of the picture was the manor house. It belonged to Sir Robert Percy who was the owner of Wharram Percy in the fourteenth century. He was known as the **lord** of the **manor**.

Think

- Find the manor house.
- Find the peasants' houses.
- What does the reconstruction suggest about how the peasants got their food?

Reconstruction of Wharram Percy as it might have looked in the Middle Ages

STEP 1

At the end of this enquiry you will be invited to speak at a special conference for archaeologists and historians. You are an archaeologist at Wharram Percy. Write up your findings ready for the conference. Use these headings.

Skeletons
(What do these tell us about medieval peasants?)

Aerial photograph
(What does this tell us about medieval villages? Use the reconstruction of the village to help you.)

Digs of peasant houses
(What do these tell us about how the peasants lived? Use the objects and the reconstruction of the house to help you.)

Peasants in pictures

You have found out quite a lot about medieval peasants from the objects they left behind in the ground. But there are still a lot of questions to answer. Some of the most important sources which historians use are pictures. Your family photographs or videos will be very useful for historians in the future!

Now take a closer look at some very rare and interesting pictures from the early fourteenth century. They show some of the jobs which peasants did.

All these pictures are found in a famous book called the Luttrell Psalter. The book belonged to Sir Geoffrey Luttrell. He was lord of the manor of Irnham in Lincolnshire.

Think

- What jobs are the peasants doing in each of the pictures?

- What tools and equipment are they using?

- What can these pictures tell us that the artefacts on page 8 cannot tell us?

Pictures from the Luttrell Psalter

You are a historian who has made a special study of the Luttrell Psalter. Write up your findings ready for the conference about medieval peasants. Use these headings to help you.

Different jobs

Tools and equipment

Men's work and women's work

Writing it down

The pictures from Sir Geoffrey Luttrell's psalter show that medieval peasants had to work very hard. However, the pictures do not show one very surprising thing about their work. For many days each year, some of the peasants were forced to work for their Lord **for nothing**.

The peasants were either **freemen** or **villeins**.

FREEMEN

We work for ourselves.

We can leave the manor if we want.

We pay rent to the Lord for our land.

VILLEINS

We spend some days each week working on the Lord's land.

We need the Lord's permission to leave the manor.

We have to do extra work for the Lord at harvest time.

Think

● Which group of peasants had to work for their lord for nothing?

Twice a year villeins and freemen were forced to attend the manorial court. This was usually held in the manor house. It was here that the steward made sure that the peasants obeyed the rules of the manor. The court records can tell us a lot about the ways in which the peasants were under the lord's control. You can see some manorial court records in this picture. They were written in Latin on great rolls of parchment.

Here are some extracts from the court records of the manor of Chatteris in Cambridgeshire. For a time in the fourteenth century the manor was owned by a woman, the Abbess of Chatteris.

Manorial court records

Robert Leger ran away. It is ordered to take his four and a half acres of barley to the Lady's hall and arrest him when he is found.

Matilda Nutrex brewed and sold ale in her house. Fined 6d.

Richard Brun pays the Lady for permission for his daughter to marry.

They say that Henry Swan's son has become a priest without permission. Fined 4d.

Henry Atthil ploughed a footpath. Fined 2d.

William Barrington set fish traps in private waters. Fined 1d.

Henry Tucker refused to thresh the Lady's corn. Fined 6d.

William Barly, Beatrix Goss, Alan Asselote and Henry Werry each fined 3d because they did not take care with their carts.

Matilda, daughter of Ate, fornicated with Richard Legat. Fined 6d.

Extracts from manorial court records of the manor of Chatteris, fourteenth century

Think

- In what ways were the peasants under the Abbess of Chatteris' control?

- What can these court records tell us that the pictures and artefacts **cannot** tell us?

You are a historian who has made a special study of the manorial court records of the manor of Chatteris. Write up your findings ready for the conference on medieval peasants.

Explain what the Chatteris records tell us about the lives of medieval peasants. Use these headings to help you.

<u>Freemen and villeins</u>

<u>Manorial courts</u>

<u>How the abbess of Chatteris controlled her peasants</u>

Thinking your enquiry through

It's now time for your conference.

1 Some people in your class should be archaeologists and others should be historians.

2 Use your notes from either Step 1, Step 2 or Step 3 to work out what you will say at the conference.

3 At the end of the conference you should decide to meet again in three year's time. Make a table like this one to show the questions you still want to ask about medieval peasants. Here are some to start you off.

Questions about medieval peasants	Evidence you might use
Did peasants enjoy themselves?	Pictures of peasants playing games
What did peasants eat?	Archaeological evidence: pots, rubbish tips
Who was in charge in peasants' villages?	
Why did so many peasant children die?	

Family fortresses

What can a castle's story tell us about medieval minds?

This is Chepstow Castle, the oldest stone castle in Britain. Look very carefully at the rectangular tower towards the back of the photograph. This was the first part of the castle to be built. It is a **hall-keep**.

It was built as a sign of power. This was the place where the lord of the castle met his followers. The very first stones of this hall-keep were laid in 1067.

Your enquiry

The story of this castle is much more than the story of a pile of stones. It will tell you all sorts of things about powerful medieval people. It will tell you what they thought was important and what hopes and fears they had. But you need to bring the castle to life again. You need to hear the story of the castle from the point of view of the people who built it. By the end of this enquiry you will be able to answer the question, 'What does the story of Chepstow Castle tell you about medieval minds?'

Chepstow 1: the castle of William fitz Osbern

It is 1068. It is now two years since the Battle of Hastings. William the Conqueror has been acting quickly.

William always knew that the Battle of Hastings was only the start. Since then, he has been giving large parcels of English land to his most trusted Norman lords. These powerful men have been building castles on their lands. Only the strongest and safest castles will do. This is very important wherever the English are rebellious and difficult. It is even more important on the edges of William's new kingdom. He has heard that wild, strange people live there. They are called the Welsh. These people might be a danger to Norman rule.

William the Conqueror has always trusted his old friend William fitz Osbern. A few months after the Battle of Hastings, he rewarded him by making him the Earl of Hereford. But William the Conqueror wants something in return. William fitz Osbern must use his lands as a base for conquering the Welsh kingdom of Gwent.

15

William fitz Osbern begins building his castle very quickly. He has chosen to build the castle out of stone. Other Norman lords are building castles of wood, but William fitz Osbern is impatient. He knows that Chepstow is in a dangerous position. There is no time to lose.

He has instructed his builders to create a large **bailey** or yard where soldiers can live in times of unrest. Here he can keep horses, food and weapons too. Now, in 1068, his castle looks like this.

Chepstow 1

William fitz Osbern has great hopes for Chepstow. He wants to stay loyal to the king, but he has a few ideas of his own. He hopes that his family will be the most powerful one in these parts. He knows that he, and his sons after him, can become very powerful in these western lands.

Think

- What do you think the buildings in the bailey are for?
- How will the soldiers spot attackers approaching in the distance?
- Which parts of the castle do you think might be weakest in time of attack?

What he does not know is that he will die in battle in 1071. Worse still, his son, Roger, will rebel against the king. His family will have to give up all their lands to the king as a punishment. William would be horrified to discover that in 1115 King Henry I will grant Chepstow to a completely different family, the de Clares.

Chepstow 2: the castle of William Marshal

It is now 1210. It is 139 years since William fitz Osbern died. William Marshal is the proud owner of Chepstow Castle and all the lands of the de Clares. William is very pleased with himself. He is only a knight. Yet his hard work and his loyalty to the king have brought fine rewards.

William Marshal fought bravely in France. He was also very wise to remain loyal to King Henry II. Many powerful families deserted Henry II, but William Marshal did not. He has been well rewarded. Henry II's son, the great King Richard, gave William a magnificent prize for his loyalty. William Marshal still cannot believe his good fortune.

As his reward, the king told him to marry a very wealthy heiress from a rich family. People called her 'the Maid of Chepstow'. She was Isabella de Clare.

William Marshal was already an experienced castle-builder and he knew exactly what to do. He had already built this magnificent round **keep** at Pembroke Castle.

Think

- Why was King Richard so pleased with William Marshal?

- How did William come to own Chepstow Castle?

He knew that Chepstow needed similar improvements. After all, it had stood unchanged for nearly a century and a half!

In 1210, Chepstow looks like this.

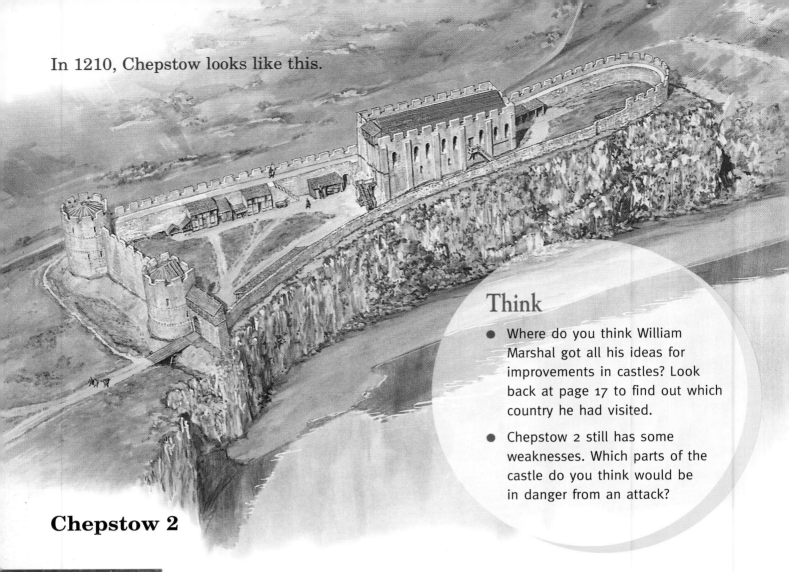

Chepstow 2

Think

- Where do you think William Marshal got all his ideas for improvements in castles? Look back at page 17 to find out which country he had visited.

- Chepstow 2 still has some weaknesses. Which parts of the castle do you think would be in danger from an attack?

STEP 1

Look carefully at the picture of Chepstow in 1210. Find each of these changes:

tower   **arrow slits**
new wall   **entrance.**

How do you think each of these changes would have improved the defences of the castle?

William is confident that he has made Chepstow strong and safe. He has also built another castle near Chepstow, at Usk. Now the border lands should be safe from the Welsh.

William Marshal has five healthy sons. Of course, he must not be too hopeful for the future. Sons are always dying in battles and from diseases, which is why it is a good idea to have lots of them. But he is confident that his sons will stay loyal to the king and will continue to improve Chepstow's defences.

William Marshal is lucky. After his death, each one of his five sons will inherit the castle in turn. William Marshal cannot begin to guess how much Chepstow will change. By the time his youngest son, Anselm, has finished with it, the castle will be almost unrecognisable. Chepstow is about to be transformed.

Chepstow 3: the castle of the younger Marshals

It is now 1244. Only one of William Marshal's five sons is still alive. Anselm Marshal often walks around the castle enjoying the fine craftmanship and masonry of his castle. The rich purple-red sandstone of the newer parts of the castle glows in the sunlight. This type of stone is much cheaper than the creamy yellow limestone which his father and elder brothers used. How foolish they were to pay for it to be brought all the way from Bristol.

The sandstone is cheap because it can be found locally. Anselm often wonders what his father would think if he saw the castle now. So many changes have been made that it is hard to remember which part was built by which brother.

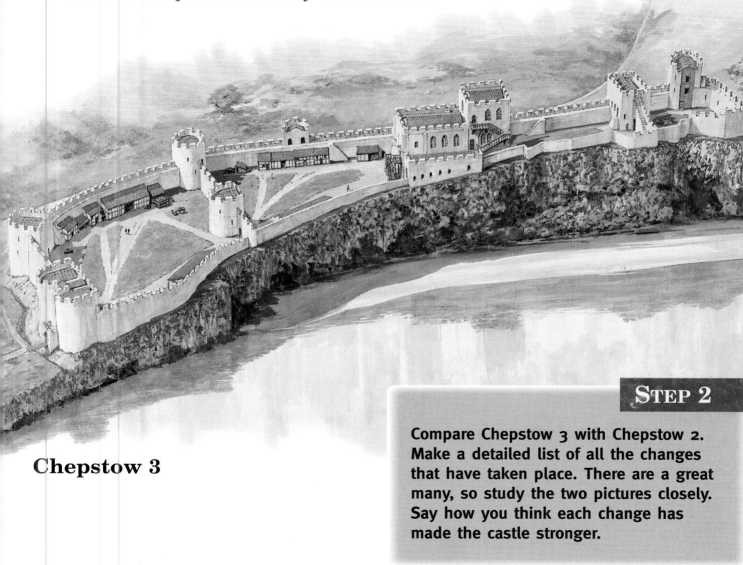

Chepstow 3

STEP 2

Compare Chepstow 3 with Chepstow 2. Make a detailed list of all the changes that have taken place. There are a great many, so study the two pictures closely. Say how you think each change has made the castle stronger.

The castle was also made more comfortable to live in. In 1228 the eldest of William Marshal's sons (also called William Marshal, just to confuse you!) received a gift from the king of ten oak trees. William used this gift to rebuild the old hall-keep and to turn it into a fine tower. The windows were made much larger and beautiful arches were built. This reconstruction shows what the tower might have looked like inside.

This is what the inside of the great tower looks like today.

An artist's reconstruction of the inside of the tower in 1240

Think

● Find the holes in the walls of the ruined building where the oak beams fitted.

● The artist has had to use the ruined building to help make the picture of the reconstruction. Match up other details from the ruined building with the artist's reconstruction.

The youngest of the five Marshal brothers, Anselm Marshal, will die in 1245. Like his four brothers before him, he will die childless. So this is the end of the Marshal's family line. However, the Marshals have some sisters. The eldest sister, Maud, will inherit the castle and when she dies will pass it to her son, Roger Bigod, the Earl of Norfolk.

Chepstow 4: the castle of Roger Bigod III

It is now 1300. Roger Bigod III is the owner of the castle. The Bigods are very grand nobles. They have other lands too, in places as far away as East Anglia. They are richer and more important than the Marshals and they want everyone to know it.

Roger Bigod III is now an old man. He is glad of the comfortable living conditions in the newest part of the castle. However, he is worried. Over the last 30 years he has turned Chepstow Castle into a home fit for a fine **nobleman**, but he has spent far too much money.

Even so, when he looks back on all the changes he has made, he has no regrets. The first thing he did was to strengthen the upper gatehouse in the **barbican** with a gate tower and **portcullis**.

He also built a wall around the whole of Chepstow. While King Edward I was busy finishing off the conquest of Wales, there were several Welsh revolts. Roger could not be too careful. Chepstow needed the protection of a strong wall. He also hired a military engineer to advise him about placing catapults on four of the towers.

Think

- Which of the four towers do you think Roger's engineer chose for his catapults? Why?

- How do you think that the four separate baileys or yards would help to keep the castle safer during attack?

- Chepstow Castle was never involved in any fighting during the Middle Ages. Why then do you think that Roger Bigod carried on improving its defences?

Chepstow 4

Roger Bigod III also built a fine hall range with kitchens and cellars and grand apartments. He had many servants and they all needed to live somewhere in the castle.

This photograph was taken from inside the lower bailey, facing the hall range.

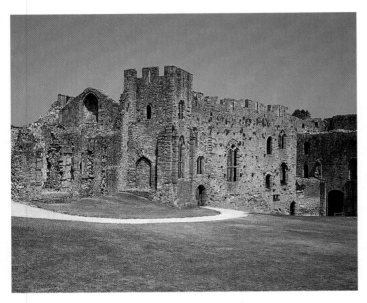

Think

- What are the signs that this was a very grand part of the castle?

- What clues can you see which might help you to work out the position of walls and floors?

The tower in the south-east corner of the same bailey has also been smartened up and made fit for important visitors. Finally, the great tower has changed, yet again. It is certainly very different now from William fitz Osbern's old keep of 1068! Back in the eleventh century everyone would have lived together. Now, the castle had separate buildings for the baron and the top men in the household as well as lodgings for guests and their servants.

Life in the castle was very good if you were the earl or one of his friends. Earl Roger liked a good feast. These pictures were made in the fourteenth century. They can give you clues about how food was served by servants. Roger Bigod III would have had lots of servants.

STEP 3

Use the picture of Chepstow 4 and all you have read to make two lists under these headings:

How the castle was made more comfortable to live in

How the castle was made stronger

In 1302 Roger Bigod III will solve his money problem. He will make an agreement with the king, Edward I. The king will give Earl Roger a sum of money every year. In return, the castle will pass to the king when Roger dies. By the time he dies in 1306, Edward I will have conquered Wales. After this, Chepstow will no longer have any military importance.

During the fourteenth and fifteenth centuries Chepstow will sometimes be in the hands of noblemen, sometimes the king. Sometimes it will become a hiding place for noblemen fleeing from trouble, sometimes for kings fleeing from noblemen. But no major building works will be carried out. Chepstow is no longer worth the trouble.

Thinking your enquiry through

1   Make a table like this one. Fill in as many details as you can from all the writing and all the pictures.

	1068	1210	1244	1300
Who owned the castle? (Don't just list names. Say what kind of family they came from.)				
How had they come to own it? (Had they inherited it, gained it by marriage or received it as a reward?)				
What do they want to use Chepstow for? (To show off? To use as a base for attack? To keep English lands safe? To please the king?)				
How strong is it? (What improvements have been made to the castle defences?)				
How comfortable is it to live in? (Look closely at all the pictures and the writing.)				

2   What does the story of Chepstow Castle tell you about the power struggles of noblemen and kings?
(*Think about how the castle was used as a reward for loyalty; how the castle was meant to help the Normans to increase their power; and how its owners used the castle as a sign of wealth and power.*)

3   What does this castle's story tell you about medieval minds?
(*Think about the hopes and fears of kings; and the hopes and fears of knights and noblemen.*)

'The most terrible of all terrors'

What makes a good story about the Black Death?

It is August 1348. In the village of Melton the day's work is ending. William Brewer puts his scythe over his shoulder and heads for home. For the last four days all the villeins on the manor of Melton have been harvesting the Bishop of Winchester's wheat. William looks at the evening sky. He is pleased. One more fine day will finish the bishop's work. Then he will bring in his own grain.

William walks slowly down the dusty track which leads to the village. He passes the dismal house of Mad Agnes, the lonely old woman some people say is a witch. The door is open, a fire smokes, but the house is empty.

As William enters the village he sees a small group of people standing in front of the church. They are listening to Hugh Barley, the Melton carpenter. Their faces are troubled. Hugh is back from Winchester where he is helping to build the new **cathedral**. He has returned with strange and worrying news.

Winchester is full of rumours of a terrible **plague** which is sweeping through Europe. People say the plague started in the east when frogs, snakes and scorpions fell from the sky. They say it is spread by the wind. No one can escape. In the towns and villages of Europe bodies lie in the streets. There is no one to bury the dead. The smell of rotting corpses is everywhere. People avoid each other. Parents run away from their children.

William listens but does not believe. Hugh is always returning from Winchester with wild stories. No wonder it is taking so long to build that cathedral! By the time William reaches his cottage he has forgotten the stories. It is almost dark now. Above the fire the evening meal simmers in the pot. His wife, Mary, is carding wool by the fire. His three children sleep soundly on a pile of straw in the corner. William sits down to eat with his wife.

Seven weeks later William Brewer will be eating alone. The villagers of Melton never finished the harvest in 1348. By the end of September the crops lay rotting in the fields. All work had stopped on Winchester Cathedral. Mad Agnes had been stoned to death. William Brewer's wife and three children lay in a shallow grave in Melton

Your enquiry

This story is made up. William Brewer and the village of Melton did not really exist. However, the story is based on what really happened. The Black Death killed millions. It was the most terrible thing which happened to people in the Middle Ages. In this enquiry you will find out how this horrible disease changed people's lives. You will use the facts to write your own historical story about what happened to William Brewer and the people of Melton.

The plague arrives

Historians think that the plague arrived in England during the summer of 1348. During the following autumn it spread quickly through the south west. Few villages escaped. The churchyards soon filled up with bodies. At night the dead were piled on carts and taken to new burial grounds.

The plague spread quickly in the warm winter of 1348–9. The next summer the people of the north of England and Wales watched in horror as their families and friends died around them. By 1350 nearly the whole of Britain was infected. At the end of that year nearly two and a half million people were dead.

A terrible death

Medieval people did not know how the disease was spread. They were puzzled as they watched their loved ones die a terrible death.

Day 1 Painful swellings called buboes appeared in the victim's armpits and groin. These were usually about the size of an egg, but could sometimes be as big as an apple.

Day 2 The victim vomited and developed a fever.

Day 3 Bleeding under the skin caused dark blotches all over the body.

Day 4 The disease attacked the nervous system. This caused the victim to suffer spasms. The victim was in terrible pain.

Day 5 Sometimes the buboes burst and a foul-smelling black liquid oozed from the open boils. When this happened the victim usually lived. However, in most cases the victim suffered a painful death.

Causes and cures

We now know that the most common form of the Black Death was bubonic plague. This disease was spread by fleas which lived on the black rat. The fleas sucked the rat's blood which contained the plague germs. When the rat died the fleas jumped on to humans and passed on the deadly disease.

Medieval people did not know about germs causing disease. They did not understand that plague was spread by rats and fleas. They thought that people's bodies were poisoned.

If the swellings burst and the poison came out people sometimes survived. It therefore seemed sensible to draw out the poison. Here are two cures from medieval medical books:

The swellings should be softened with figs and cooked onions. The onions should be mixed with yeast and butter. Then open the swellings with a knife.

Take a live frog and put its belly on the plague sore. The frog will swell up and burst. Keep doing this with further frogs until they stop bursting. Some people say that a dried toad will do the job better.

STEP 1

Now start your story of what happened when the plague reached Melton.

1 Decide who the first plague victims will be. You can make up characters or use some of the people in the story on pages 24 and 25.

2 Describe how the people suffered and what cures their families tried.

3 Try to include lots of detail about medieval village life to make the opening of your story interesting and accurate.

Fears and ideas

To medieval people the Black Death must have seemed like the end of the world. People were desperate. Different people had different ideas about what should be done. Here, people are punishing themselves with whips.

This picture shows people whipping themselves in Rome. The Black Death was feared all over Europe.

Think

- List all the the things which show that the people in the picture were very religious.

- Why did people think that by whipping themselves they would make the plague go away?

People whipping themselves in Rome. A fifteenth-century picture

What people believed

The evil planets of Mars and Saturn have moved closer together. This has turned the air bad. If we breath in the bad air we will catch the plague.

God has sent the plague because he is angry with us. We have spent too much time gambling, fighting and drinking.

The plague passes from person to person. Plague sores give off a terrible smell. If you breath this in you will catch the plague.

What people did

You should carry a bunch of herbs and hold it to your nostrils at all times.

They say that the Bishop of Winchester has run away.

We need to bury the clothes of the plague victims.

Thousands of people are going on pilgrimage to Canterbury, Walsingham and other holy places.

You should not go near stagnant water, slaughter houses or rubbish heaps.

The sick should be forced to leave the village.

Some people burn sweet-smelling wood in their houses.

They say that in London people walk through the streets singing hymns and whipping each other to show how sorry they are.

We need to pray to God and ask him to forgive us.

We need to burn the clothes of the plague victims.

STEP 2

1   To work out why medieval people did these things we need to match their actions to what they believed. Make a table like this and put the things people did in the correct column.

Sent by God	Bad Air	Person to Person
	bury clothes	

2   Now write the second part of your story. Many people are dying and the villagers meet in the church to decide what to do. What does William Brewer say at the meeting? Do other people share his views? What happens in the village as more and more people die of the plague?

The survivors

Historians think that just over half the population survived the Black Death. Life was never the same again. People had suffered the terrible fear and horror of the plague years. This fear did not go away. Pictures like this one became very common in the years after the Black Death.

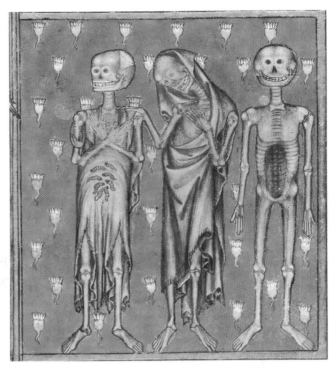

A detail from 'The three living and the three dead'.
A fourteenth-century picture

Think

- What does this picture show?

- How did the Black Death affect the way medieval people thought?

The fear stayed, but for many survivors everyday life got better.

Wages and prices

BEFORE THE PLAGUE

After the plague, prices of food and other goods fell. The shortage of labourers meant that wages went up. In 1351 the government passed a law to keep wages low. This was called the **Statute of Labourers**. It said that labourers should not earn more than 2d a day. The law did not work. The lords needed labourers and they were forced to pay high wages for them.

AFTER THE PLAGUE

More land

Some villages lost nearly all their people. Many were completely abandoned. In other villages the survivors were able to buy or rent all the spare land. So some peasants became much richer.

The end of labour services

Most peasants were villeins. These people were forced to work on the lord's land for 40 days each year, without payment! After the Black Death the lords were short of labourers, so the peasants could bargain with them. This helped to free the peasants from the lord's control. Many left their manors.

A better standard of living

Because of all these changes many peasants were better off. They were able to rebuild their houses making them bigger and more comfortable. They ate more meat and less bread. They even began to wear clothes made of coloured material.

STEP 3

It's time to finish your story about William Brewer and the other survivors of the plague at Melton.

Use the information in the section called 'The survivors' to explain what happened to him and the other peasants in the years after the Black Death.

Thinking your enquiry through

How good is your historical story?
Of course, it is made up. But if it is a really good historical story, it will be based upon lots of facts about the Black Death.

1 Take a red pen. Underline in red all the parts of your story which are based upon **facts** about how horrible the disease was.

2 Take a green pen. Underline in green all the parts of your story which are based on what medieval people **thought** about the Black Death.

3 Take a black pen. Underline in black all the parts of the story which are based upon the **effects** which the Black Death had upon peasants and villages. For example, did William Brewer become freer? Was he able to escape the lord's control?

Perhaps you found that you did not have very much to underline in some of these colours. Now you know how to go back and make your historical story even better.

'Only a townsman ...' ④

Did the towns make people free?

You are a villein, living miserably in the countryside under the control of your lord. You have had enough. There is only one way to get free. You will have to run away.

It will be risky. The lord will do his best to find you. So you must run to a town. You have heard from the travelling **pedlars** that towns are places of freedom. You can get lost in a town. They are full of outsiders anyway. But some towns are extra safe. Some towns have made special rules to protect runaway villeins. Here is an example.

Royal Charter to Gloucester, 1227

If any villein should stay in the town and support himself and pay his taxes for a year and a day, after that time he cannot be caught again by his lord.

Phew! Made it!

It had not always been like this. For many years after 1066 all towns belonged to the local landowner – a Norman **baron**, a **bishop**, or the king himself. The local landowner could force the townsmen to work on his land. He could charge them rent and stop them from leaving the town. He could treat the townspeople as badly as he treated the villeins who lived in the village! But the merchants and craftspeople who lived in the towns wanted to be free.

> We need to buy and sell land in the town.

> We need to turn our market stalls into proper shops.

> We need to make agreements with each other about prices.

Bit by bit, as towns became richer, townspeople were able to buy their freedom from the landowner. This is why many history books tell the story of medieval towns as the story of people becoming free.

Your enquiry

Just how free were the people who lived in these towns? When the lord was no longer in charge, who was in charge in his place? Was one person as free as another person? By the end of this enquiry you will be able to decide for yourself how free the townspeople were.

Whenever people get together in groups they start to make rules. Medieval towns were full of rules. There were rules to make things fair and rules to make things safe. There were rules to keep people free and rules to keep the town strong. Thinking about rules is a good way to start thinking about medieval towns.

Keeping up the standard

Buying and selling

Between 1100 and 1300 more and more food was produced. Peasants who grew any spare food took it to a local market. Many of these markets grew into towns. Towns were places for buying and selling.

This picture shows a shop selling clothes.

Townspeople needed all sorts of rules to stop disagreements. Here are some pieces of evidence which describe rules made about buying and selling:

Think

- The two people in the picture seem to be arguing. What kinds of things might they be arguing about?

No fish is to be sold after vespers or before the bell is rung for the first church service on the next day.

Town laws of York, 1301

Each baker is to have his own sign for baking his bread.

Town laws of York, 1301

John Penrose was accused of selling wine which was bad. John Penrose is found guilty. He must drink a large amount of his bad wine. The rest of the wine will be poured over his head.

London, 1364

Making things

Towns needed not only shops, but work-shops. As towns grew in size, different crafts grew up. It was not enough just to make rules about buying and selling. People also needed rules about how goods were to be made.

The town **guilds** were the big rule-makers. Guilds made the rules about who was allowed to practise a craft and what sorts of standards should be kept. The guilds became very powerful. By the fourteenth century it was almost impossible to work at a craft without belonging to the guild.

If you wanted to learn a craft you had to become an **apprentice**, usually for seven years. At the end of the seven years your work would be examined by a guild master to check if it was good enough. The rules of the guild were very strict.

This picture shows two apprentices having their work examined by a guild master.

A medieval painting of a guild master

If your work was good enough you became a journeyman for another seven years. After that, if you were really, really good, you too could become a master. This involved producing a perfect piece of work – a 'masterpiece'.

The guilds wanted to keep prices high. They wanted to stop outsiders from coming in and offering goods for lower prices. Guilds also made all sorts of rules to stop too many goods from being produced. The last thing they wanted was competition. This would take away their control and lower the standards of the craft.

The wiremakers of Shrewsbury made this rule in 1481:

No person is allowed to work after 9 pm. It will annoy people with the noise of knocking and filing. If he does, he will be fined one pound of wax or 8d.

Shrewsbury Wiremakers' Guild, 1481

Think

● Apart from the noise, can you think of any other reasons why a guild might not want people to work at night?

Sometimes the guilds used their power to keep out certain types of townspeople whom they did not like or who they thought were wicked or strange. They also kept women out.

Medieval people saw silk-making, spinning and brewing as women's work. But women also worked as ironmongers, shoe-makers and goldsmiths. Some guilds allowed women to practise a craft, but would not let women become full guild members. Some barbers' and dyers' guilds accepted women, but most guilds kept them out altogether.

Here is one set of town laws:

> If any married woman follow a craft within the city, which her husband has nothing to do with, she shall be counted as a sole (unmarried) woman in matters to do with her craft. And if a complaint is made against her, she shall answer it as a sole woman.

Town laws of Lincoln

Goodies from the guilds

The guilds used their wealth to do wonderful things for towns. They put on feasts, processions and plays. The Guild of Mercers (dealers in cloth) in London charged 6d a week and used the money to help members who were poor or sick. Guilds sometimes ran homes for old people and paid for the funerals of poor guild members. As towns and trade grew, some wealthy guildsmen wanted a better education for their sons (but not for their daughters!). Sometimes guilds set money aside to buy books or to employ a schoolmaster.

Having a guild was great ...
as long as you were in it.

Think

- Why was the guild so keen to control the people who practised each craft?
- Why do you think that the guilds wanted to keep women out?

STEP 1

You now need to make one big point summing up the section called 'Keeping up the standard'. You must do this in just one sentence!

1 Choose the **best** sentence summary below and write it out. Three do not get it quite right or do not give the full picture.

- The guilds stopped people from making and selling any goods.
- Anyone could make and sell goods in medieval times.
- The guilds controlled the making and sale of goods very tightly.
- The guilds made so many rules that no one liked them.

You can make up a better summary if you can, but it must be just one sentence.

2 Now make a rough list of a few little points or examples which you could use to back up your sentence. You will need points on the rules about buying and selling, apprentices and masters, and guilds.

Keeping people in order

I, Earl Roger, grant the townsmen freedom to run their own affairs

Town councils

As towns grew richer in the twelfth and thirteenth centuries, they started to gain freedom from the king and his nobles. The chief townsmen would offer to buy a **charter** for a large sum of money. Then they were released from the lord's control and became 'freemen' of the city. A charter gave them the right to buy and sell land and to elect a town **council**.

The town council contained the town's most important men. They made laws about every aspect of town life. In 1298 the City of York's rules covered food hygiene, the behaviour of doctors, drains, public toilets, prostitutes and wandering pigs.

This picture is taken from a charter to the town of Bristol in 1347. The first scene shows two people being locked up for breaking the law. The second scene shows a baker being dragged through the streets.

Think

- What do the scales above the baker's head suggest about what the baker has done wrong?

This picture shows a new mayor of Bristol swearing to keep the laws of the town. Notice how all the people in the picture look very rich and important.

Edward III's charter to Bristol, 1347

A mayor-making ceremony in Bristol. A fifteenth-century picture

Medieval towns could be places which welcomed and accepted all kinds of people, even people from different religions and different countries. Medieval English people could also turn on the outsiders and be terrifyingly cruel.

A terrible tale of tragedy in London and York

During the reign of Henry II a small community of Jews settled in York. Two of the Jews were important townsmen – Benedict and Josce. They had become rich by lending money to northern landowners.

In 1189 King Richard I was to be crowned. Both these important men decided to travel to London for the great occasion.

Many people in London did not like the Jews. They thought that the Jews brought strange and wicked customs to the city. They were jealous of their success. Benedict and Josce found themselves in London at just the wrong time. While they were there a terrible riot took place. Benedict was killed.

Josce escaped quickly, but the journey home was dangerous. Riots were now spreading to other English towns. He longed to get back to York. When he got there, things were no better. Some of the Yorkshire landowners owed the Jews money. They had been encouraging the ordinary people of York to hate the Jews. Before Josce could rush to protect them, a mob killed Benedict's wife and all his children.

Josce thought quickly. He gathered together all the Jews and fled to York Castle for safety. The Jews' leader, Rabbi Yemtob, encouraged his people to commit suicide. Many did. Those who did not kill themselves were promised that they would be freed, but on one condition. They would have to be baptised as Christians. The terrified Jews agreed, in the hope of saving their lives. But the mob broke their promise and killed them anyway.

Think

- Why did the people of London and York became angry with the Jews?

- The Jews lived peacefully in these towns before. What do you think might have caused some people to turn against them?

40

1   You now need to make **one big point** summing up the section called 'Keeping people out'. Choose the best summary sentence from the list below.

- Towns were terrified of outsiders and always kept them out.
- Townspeople needed outsiders for trade and welcomed anyone to visit, live or work in the town.
- Towns kept out Jews, Scots and women, but let everyone else in.

- Towns were places where outsiders came to trade and where people could gain freedom from a lord, but outsiders were sometimes mistrusted, treated cruelly or kept out.

2   Now select some **little points**. You will need little points on invaders and strangers, and on the special examples from York and London.

Thinking your enquiry through

You are now going to answer the question, 'How free were the townspeople?'

You are going to write an essay. It will have five paragraphs (or more if you like).

To help you the introduction (your first paragraph) has been written for you. You can either copy this out or write a better one.

Your introduction

The story of medieval towns is the story of English people becoming free. After 1100 many towns bought charters to give them their freedom. Villeins who stayed in a town for a year and a day could become free from their lord. These were very important developments. However, there are different kinds of freedom. Some groups enjoyed more freedom than others.

Your second, third and fourth paragraphs

Begin your second, third and fourth paragraphs with the sentences that you chose in Steps 1, 2 and 3. Complete each of these paragraphs with a few ideas, facts or examples (your little points).

Your conclusion

Try to sum up your views on:
- the ways in which townspeople were free
- the ways in which the freedom of different types of people was limited.

Invaders

Why did the Normans win the Battle of Hastings?

The invaders get ready

Look carefully at these pictures. They all show people getting ready for a very special event in a very important year, 1066.

Here men are chopping down trees to build ships.

Here they are dragging the ships to the sea.

Now the boats are carrying horses across the sea.

Here they are carrying armour, weapons and supplies to the sea.

These pictures are from the Bayeux tapestry. The tapestry tells one of the most famous stories of British history, the story of the Normans' victory over the English at the Battle of Hastings.

These pictures show the preparations. The Normans went to an awful lot of trouble. This is not surprising. Their leader William, Duke of Normandy, was absolutely determined to invade England. In 1066 he did.

Britain had been invaded many times before. She had been invaded by Romans, Saxons, Angles and Vikings. But the Norman invasion was special. Earlier invasions were only waves of settlers. William had plans to take over the whole of England.

The battle had big results for England, and later for Wales and Scotland too. If things had turned out differently, the course of British history might have been different. In fact, **it very nearly was ...**

Your enquiry

Historians like to work out **why** things happen. They try to explain things. When we look for the causes of the Norman victory we find some surprising things. William was very skilful, and determined, but he was also very lucky.

So why did the Normans win the battle of Hastings? You are going to build your very own historical explanation.

William was determined

William knew that it would be difficult. His advisers knew that it would be difficult too. In 1071 William's chaplain (priest) wrote about an argument which he remembered William having with his barons:

> Some of the greatest lords of Normandy argued with Duke William against the idea of sending an army to England. They said that it was too difficult and would cost more than Normandy could afford.

But William was determined. He was not going to let anyone stop him.

STEP 1

Here are three causes of the Normans' success. Copy each one carefully on to small pieces of paper.

> The Normans had knights on horseback who were skilful fighters.

> The Normans prepared carefully. They brought with them a useful mixture of well-equipped foot-soldiers, archers and cavalry.

> William was skilful, ambitious and determined to be King of England.

What do these three causes have in common? Make up one heading to sum up all three cards.

The English were not ready

Harold

In 1066, King Harold of England was in big trouble. He had only just become king. The old king, Edward the Confessor, had died without children. Harold was a very important earl and very good leader in battles. So, on the day of Edward's funeral, important Englishmen chose him as king.

The trouble was, three other people wanted to be King of England too.

Tostig

Harald Hardraada

William

Harold's spies told him that the Normans were preparing. Harold knew that William and the Normans would come. Harold gathered the largest army ever seen in England. All summer he kept his fleet along the coast, waiting and waiting for the Normans to come.

Harold waited ... and waited and waited. William did not sail. William **could not** set sail. Until the right wind blew, it was impossible.

Suddenly Harold had terrible news. Harald Hardraada, King of Norway, had landed in the north. Worse still, Tostig had joined him. Harold had to forget about William. He needed to go north.

The map shows what happened next.

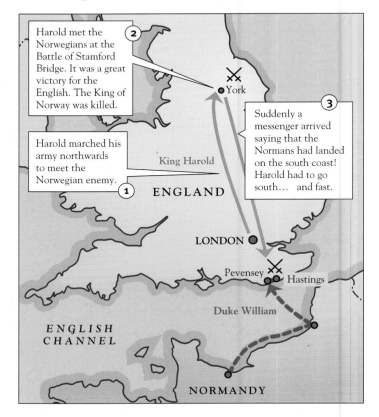

Harold met the Norwegians at the Battle of Stamford Bridge. It was a great victory for the English. The King of Norway was killed. **2**

Harold marched his army northwards to meet the Norwegian enemy. **1**

Suddenly a messenger arrived saying that the Normans had landed on the south coast! Harold had to go south… and fast. **3**

York

King Harold

ENGLAND

LONDON

Pevensey Hastings

Duke William

ENGLISH CHANNEL

NORMANDY

His men were exhausted, but Harold galloped on and on. Many of his foot-soldiers got left behind because they could not keep up.

Meanwhile, the Normans had found time to gather food, and to build a secure camp. Harold met the Normans at Hastings. Harold had always been a good leader in battle, but this time, he **was not ready**.

Here are four more causes of the Normans' success. Copy each one carefully on to small pieces of paper:

The wind changed and allowed William's troops to cross the channel at a time when Harold's troops were away in the north.

Some of Harold's best fighters died at the Battle of Stamford Bridge.

Stamford Bridge and the journey south made Harold's troops very tired.

The battle began before Harold's troops were properly ready.

Make up one heading to sum up all four cards.

The battle

The Bayeux tapestry shows Harold's soldiers all squashed together on top of a hill. William of Poitiers' writings also give evidence that the English were grouped together to make a kind of wall with their shields.

Here is the scene from the Bayeux tapestry showing the shield wall.

Here is part of William of Poitiers' description.

In front, William placed foot-soldiers with handbows and crossbows; next, more heavily armed footmen with chain mail; and finally his knights. Harold's soldiers drew up on higher ground, bunched closely together. William's men came slowly up the hill. The terrible sound of trumpets started the battle. The Norman foot-soldiers rained death on the English with their spears and arrows. The English fought bravely.

Think

- What clever decisions did both William and Harold make?

- How can you tell that the tapestry-makers probably used William of Poitier's account to help them make their pictures?

We cannot be absolutely certain, but the evidence suggests that the rest of the story goes something like this.

The Normans kept on charging up the slope and hurling their spears, but the English threw  their spears back or hacked the Normans down with their battle axes.

After a while there was a rumour that William had been killed. Some of the Normans were terrified and began to flee. But William was not dead. He pulled up his helmet and shouted: "Look at me well! I am alive and by God's grace I shall yet be victor! What is this madness that makes you flee?"

These events gave the Normans an idea. They would play a trick on the English. They decided that they would pretend to flee. That did it. The Norman trick worked. The English left their safe hilltop and hurtled down the hill after the Normans. The Normans turned around and began to slaughter the English.

The English fought on, but soon King Harold was killed. Then they knew that there was no hope. It was an English tradition never to desert a dead leader. His best soldiers struggled on, dying bravely with their fallen king.

By about five o'clock the last few English collapsed with exhaustion or fled.

Now make your last three cause cards:

William arranged his troops carefully and used them skilfully in the battle.

The Normans' clever trick of pretending to retreat caused the English to leave their strong position on the hill.

In the middle of the battle, Harold was killed. The English were weak without their leader.

Make up one heading to sum up all three cards.

The English were defeated. The Norman victory would change Britain forever. How had this happened? Was it Norman skill?. Or were the English just unlucky? You need to build your own explanation.

Thinking your enquiry through

You now have a set of cause cards. (You can make more if you want). You have them in three groups. You have given each group a heading. These headings give you the main reasons. Or do they? There are so many ways of sorting your cards!

Put all the cards in front of you. Try these other ways of grouping them. Think hard about where the cards belong. It isn't always easy.

1 Things to do with the Normans' strength and skill
Things to do with Harold's bad luck

2 Things which happened before the battle
Things which happened during the battle

3 Things to do with the armies
Things to do with the leaders

Which is the best way to group the cards? Which do you think gives the clearest explanation of why William won the Battle of Hastings? Try to think of some other ways of working the cards, using headings of your own.

When you have chosen the best way of sorting the cards, arrange them on a large piece of paper. Label the groups. You can then choose evidence, or details from the story, to put around your cards. Arrange everything carefully. You want your explanation to be clear!

The conqueror and the conquered

What did the English think when William took control?

Here is William, Duke of Normandy,
just after winning the Battle of Hastings in 1066.

* He sent it to Harold's mother!

Your enquiry

Winning one battle was not enough to give William the whole of England. He knew that the **Anglo-Saxons** (the English) would try to drive the Normans back to France. Between 1066 and 1087 William managed to take full control, but it was not easy. In this enquiry you will learn how William took control. Then you can work out what the English thought about it.

Taking the land

William left Hastings shortly after the battle. He moved his armies around the south east of England, capturing important towns along the way. Then he moved towards London from the north. The map shows the route that William took.

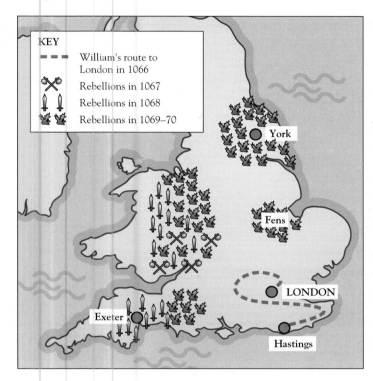

KEY

- - - William's route to London in 1066

Rebellions in 1067

Rebellions in 1068

Rebellions in 1069–70

York

Fens

LONDON

Exeter

Hastings

He told the army to burn and destroy the countryside as it approached the city. The English leaders came out to meet him. They surrendered straightaway. They promised to serve William as their king. On Christmas Day in 1066 William was crowned King of England at West-minster Abbey, but there was fighting on the streets even while the service went on. William knew that his problems were not over.

Hmm… getting crowned certainly hasn't solved all my problems. I'm going to have to get TOUGH!

Think

- Why do you think that the English leaders in London surrendered so quickly?

- In which parts of the country did William have the most trouble with rebellions?

William was right to expect trouble. Although he had killed King Harold and many English leaders at Hastings, there were others who were ready to carry on the fight. Over the next few years William had to crush many **rebellions**. The map shows where most of the rebellions took place.

William soon had serious problems in the north of England. He trusted two English earls, Edwin and Morcar, to look after that part of the country for him. When William tried to raise taxes from their land they joined forces with some Danish invaders and rose up against the Normans in 1069. They killed hundreds of Normans at York. William marched an army to the north to teach the whole area a lesson it would not forget.

William's army recaptured York and drove off the Danes. The English **rebels** fled into the countryside. William followed them. All through the bitter winter he went from village to village burning homes to the ground. This fierce punishment became known as the Harrying of the North. William's men killed the villagers' animals and destroyed their tools and supplies of food. Thousands died. Whole families starved to death. Bodies rotted at the roadside.

Here is how one **monk** described the Harrying of the North about 45 years later:

> The king stopped at nothing to hunt his enemies. He cut down many people and destroyed homes and land. Nowhere else had he shown such cruelty. To his shame he made no effort to control his fury and he punished the innocent with the guilty. He ordered that crops and herds, tools and food should be burned to ashes. More than 100,000 people perished of hunger. I have often praised William in this book, but I can say nothing good about this brutal slaughter. God will punish him.

Orderic Vitalis, early 12th century

Think

● Choose some words from this source which show what the monk thought about William and the Normans.

● One of the monk's parents was English and the other was Norman. What signs are there in the source that this monk was able to see both sides of the story?

One of the most famous rebellions of all took place in East Anglia. It was led by Hereward the Wake. For hundreds of years stories have been told about how he refused to surrender to the Normans. Here is one of the stories.

In the eleventh century the Fens were dangerous. You could look for miles and see nothing but swampy lakes and marshy rivers. Anyone who did not know the secret paths would be sucked in and drowned. In the middle of the Fens on the island of the Ely the last of the English rebels gathered. Here were the most famous fighters, so proud of the ancient stories of Anglo-Saxon bravery. The most famous of all was Hereward the Wake.

Everyone feared him. The people of the Fens said that Hereward could slaughter a strong man with his fists. They said that he could fight twelve men at once with his sword, Brainbiter, and that his horse, Swallow, was faster than any other.

This picture of Hereward was made in the nineteenth century. It shows Hereward returning to his old home which had been taken over by Normans. He is cutting down every French person in the great hall.

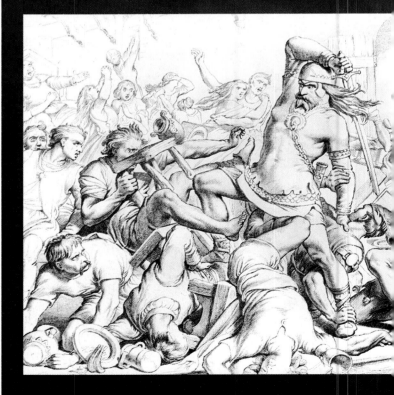

Hereward's men worked furiously, barricading the island of Ely with wooden stakes. This was the last chance for the English.

The first time the Normans came, they were not ready for the black mud of the Fens. They tried to build wooden roads across the marsh, but these soon fell into the swamp. The Normans drowned slowly in the black slime. Hereward's men celebrated. In the old abbey the English monks thanked God for victory. William tried again. This time Hereward set fire to the dry reeds. Many Normans were killed.

But William was determined. He found a way on to the island. Soon all Hereward's men were slaughtered. At the last minute, Hereward killed his horse Swallow. He preferred to let her die than see her captured by the Normans.

Think

- Why do you think that stories about Hereward were popular among English people for hundreds of years?

No one knows what happened to Hereward. There are many stories. One story says that William admired his bravery and let him go.

STEP 1

Read through the section called 'Taking the land' again. Start to make a list of reasons why many English would have hated William and his Normans. Give your list the heading 'Reasons for hating the Normans'.

Controlling the land

Wherever William's armies went they built castles. They were surprised that the English had very few of these. The Normans knew that they were outnumbered by the English so they put up castles near important river crossings or large towns. This meant that an English army could not control the countryside or move from place to place without first capturing the castle – and that was not easy.

The simplest type of castle was a **motte and bailey castle**. The Normans forced the English to build these for them. This picture shows what a motte and bailey castle might have looked like.

In larger towns and at the most important river crossings, the Normans put up stone castles. These had massive stone walls which were sometimes three metres thick. The Tower of London is the most famous of these stone castles.

This map shows where the Normans built castles between 1066 and 1086.

Think

● Use the map to work out how many castles had been built by 1086.

● Which part of the country do you think William found most difficult to control?

The Normans always tried to put their castles on the best possible sites. They often chose a place high on a rocky outcrop above a bend in a river. If the English already had houses in the best spots, the Normans simply pulled the houses down. In Lincoln, over 160 houses were destroyed to make way for the massive new Norman castle. The families who lost their houses were made homeless.

Despite this, some English people may have been grateful for the castles. The areas around them were peaceful and each castle provided work for the English. Even so, the English must have found it strange to work for Norman masters who spoke French and who looked down on them.

STEP 2

Continue the list you started in Step 1. Use information from the section called 'Controlling the land' to write down more reasons why some English would have hated the Normans.

Now start a second list. Write down any reasons why some English people might have been grateful to the Normans. Call this list 'Reasons for liking the Normans'.

Sharing out the land

As the King of England, William owned all the land in the country. However, he could not be everywhere at once. So he lent large areas of land to powerful **knights** called **barons**. These barons had to share out the land as well, so they lent smaller areas, called **manors**, to the knights. The knights were proud fighting men, not farmers, so they shared out the land on their manors among the peasants or **villeins**. It was these peasants who did the work and grew crops on the land.

When land was lent in this way it was called by a Latin word *feudum* so we call this the **feudal system**.

Of course, everyone wanted something in return for sharing out their land. Each person in the feudal system made a promise. This diagram shows the promise that each one made in return for a share of the land.

The feudal system

In this picture you can see William with his nephew, Alan of Brittany. Alan is making his promise to William. Making the promise was called **doing homage.**

Think

- How can you tell which person in the picture is William?

- Use the feudal system diagram on page 53 to work out what Alan would be saying to William.

Twelfth-century painting of William with Alan of Brittany

When William first took the throne he allowed some English earls to have land. The rebellions changed his mind. After 1071 he gave more and more land to Norman barons like Alan. By the end of William's reign in 1087 only six of the 250 great landowners in the country were English. This diagram shows how the land was divided up.

About 30 important Norman lords (many were members of William's family)

The Church
(about 50 bishops and abbots)

170 people
(only 6 were English)

As you can see from the diagram, William granted large areas of land to bishops and **abbots.** These were mostly Normans as well. William wanted to thank God for giving him victory over Harold at Hastings. He brought many new Church leaders across from Normandy. They built cathedrals in the large cities such as Durham and put up churches in towns and villages all over their new lands.

Norman churches had thick walls with solid, round pillars. The arches, windows and doors had rounded tops and were decorated with zig-zag patterns. The English were probably impressed by these strong, stone buildings because most Anglo-Saxon churches were made of wood. All over the country, ordinary English men, women and children must have seen these new churches as a sign that God had chosen to give them new masters.

This is a church built by the Normans at Iffley, near Oxford.

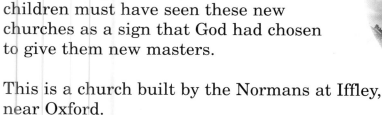

Step 3

Now look back through the section called 'Sharing out the land'.

1 Add more ideas to your first list (Reasons for hating the Normans).

2 Add more ideas to your other list (Reasons for liking the Normans).

Enjoying the land

William believed that God had given him England as a great prize. He was keen to enjoy it. He turned huge stretches of land into royal hunting estates where deer, boar and hare could run free. William used to show off his strength and skill by hunting in places such as the New Forest near Winchester. When he turned the New Forest into hunting land he pulled down over sixty villages and made the people homeless. He passed strict new laws.

Crime	Punishment
Caught hunting in royal forest	First Offence: two fingers to be chopped off Second Offence: blinded

Think

- No ruler today would get away with burning down a few villages to make a hunting forest. Why did William get away with it?

- How would chopping off two fingers stop people from hunting?

55

William changed very few laws when he became king. He simply told his barons to be strict so that the country was safe for everyone. Even the English agreed that William made their country safer in many ways.

In 1086 William decided that he needed to know just how rich his country was. So much land had changed hands since he became king that he could not be sure who owned what – or how much tax they should be paying! He was already taxing the people heavily, but he thought they could pay him more.

He sent men to over 13,000 villages. They wrote down how many people lived there, who held the land, what type of people worked on the land and even how many pigs, cows or sheep each man had. The people's answers were double-checked. Then a single monk in Winchester had to copy all the information on to **parchment**. Parchment is made from sheep's skin. The book that he produced was so long that nearly a thousand sheep were killed to make enough pages!

The people soon called it the **Domesday Book**. Here it is.

The Domesday Book

Domesday means 'God's Judgement Day'. God's judgement could not be avoided – and nor could William's taxes!

STEP 4

Use information from the section called 'Enjoying the land' to add some more ideas to your two lists.

Leaving the land

In 1087 William was fighting to capture a town in France. His horse threw him violently against the front of his saddle and he was seriously injured. A few days later, weeping and begging God to forgive him for all the blood he had shed, he died.

William had grown very fat towards the end of his life. Several monks struggled to force his enormous body into the stone coffin, but it burst open, filling the church with a foul smell. It was a remarkable end to a remarkable life.

Thinking your enquiry through

So what did the English think about William? We cannot be certain what the English thought, but we can use what we know to make sensible guesses. Some writings from the time can also help us, but again, we need to take care. The English did not write very much and the evidence which we have may not give the full picture.

1 Look carefully at the two lists which you made in the Steps. Which list is the longest? Why do you think this is?

2 Now look carefully at the two sources on this page. They were both written by Englishmen after William died. Which source best supports each list?

3 Read the two sources on the right very carefully. Match up each of the things the English wrote with things that William did. Use the ideas in your lists to help you. The first one has been done for you.

Things William did	What the English wrote about it
William commanded his barons to build castles. Sometimes whole villages were burned to make space for them.	'This King raised castles and crushed the poor.'

Source number 1

When William died in 1087 some English monks wrote down what they thought about him. They put their ideas into a book called the *Anglo-Saxon Chronicle*. Here is part of what they wrote.

> This king raised castles and crushed the poor
> He took gold and silver and so much more.
> There was no fairness in his deeds
> He simply fed his deepest greed.
> He loved to hunt for stags and boars
> He took our land and made this law:
> The eyes of poachers who steal from their Lord
> Must be cut out with the point of a sword.

Source number 2

Another Englishman wrote this:

> King William was stronger than any king before. He was gentle to the good men and stern to those who disobeyed him. Also he was very violent, so that no one dared to do anything against his will. The good peace he made in this country is not to be forgotten.
> An honest man could travel over his kingdom without injury with his pockets full of gold. William protected deer and boar and loved the stags so much as if he were their father. These things we have written about him, both good and bad, that good men may copy the good points and avoid the bad.

Blood on the cathedral floor

Why was it so difficult for kings to control the Church?

On 29 December 1170, a very important man was murdered in a very holy place. A monk called Edward Grim watched the murder. This is what he saw.

One of the knights raised his sword and wounded Becket in the head. That same blow almost cut off my arm as I held the **archbishop**. Then Becket received a second blow, but still he managed to stand. At the third blow he fell. He said, "For the name of Jesus and the protection of his Church I am prepared to die." Then the third knight struck Becket so hard that his sword broke. The top was cut off the archbishop's head so that blood stained the cathedral floor. Another man put his foot on Becket's neck and scattered his brains all over the floor. He called out, "Let us away, knights. He will trouble us no more."

Edward Grim's story of Becket's murder (1)

Think

- What was the name of the murdered man?

- Where did the murder take place?

Your enquiry

You may have seen a teacher trying to decide who was to blame for a fight. The teacher first deals with the immediate problem but then goes on to find out what lay behind it. Your enquiry is the same. The further back you go in time, the more the story starts to make sense. At the end of the enquiry you will understand how such a shocking murder came to take place. Then you can use this story to work out why it was so difficult for kings to control the Church.

Minutes before the murder

Let's go back to the events just before the murder and see what the sources say. This picture shows the murder scene.

A modern copy of a fifteenth-century painting in Canterbury Cathedral

Here is another part of the story written by the monk, Edward Grim. These words lead up to those on page 58.

The monks tried to bolt the doors to protect Becket, but he ordered them to open the doors. He said, "It is wrong to make the house of prayer into a fortress." The knights called out, "Where is Archbishop Thomas Becket, a traitor to his king and country?" Becket answered, "I am here. I am a priest of God, not a traitor. I am ready to die for Him. I will not run from your swords." The knights told Becket to forgive the people he had expelled from the Church. He refused. They tried to drag him from the cathedral, but he could not be forced away from the pillar. Then he started to lift his hands in prayer.

Edward Grim's story of Becket's murder (2)

Think

- Find the four knights, the archbishop and the monk who was with him.
- Why was this murder so shocking?

Think

- Which parts of Edward Grim's story suggest that Becket was a very religious man?
- Which parts suggest that he was a very determined man or even a stubborn man?
- Which parts suggest that he was a very brave man?

Here is another account, written by a priest called Ralph of Diceto.

On December 29th Becket was resting in his room near the cathedral. All in a fury, four knights burst into the room. They demanded, in the name of King Henry II, that the archbishop should allow the bishops he had expelled from the church to be given back their jobs. Becket said that he would only forgive them if they would swear to obey him. The knights left the room, white with anger, and hurried away to prepare their wicked plan.

Ralph of Diceto's story of Becket's murder, twelfth century

Ralph of Diceto and Edward Grim give you some clues. You need to sort them out. Find things in the sources which might fit under the following two headings:

Things which show that the archbishop had upset some bishops

Things which show that the archbishop had upset the king

But what on earth has the king got to do with it?

The king had a lot to do with it! The king at this time was Henry II. Here is a picture of King Henry II. He is with Thomas Becket. The king is on the left, with his supporters. Becket is on the right with his supporters. They are parting after a quarrel.

Becket and Henry II, painted in about 1235

You can tell that they are both angry. At this time, to point one finger was a sign of anger. King Henry II and Thomas Becket are riding away from each other after a **very** unfriendly meeting!

60

Months before the murder

You need to go further back in time to work this story out. You need to know why the king and the archbishop had not been getting on.

Read this story carefully. As you read, some things will start to make sense. There will also be some new details which will puzzle you. Make a note of any questions you have as you go along.

Thomas Becket and King Henry II met in France in July 1170. At last they patched up their quarrel. Becket agreed to return to England to serve the king. The king stayed in Normandy to look after his lands there.

 1

 2

The archbishop finally arrived back in England in December 1170. But within days he had broken his promise. He expelled from the Church all the bishops who had supported the king while he was away. He also asked the **Pope** to punish the Archbishop of York.

Some of the bishops went to see Henry in France. They told him that Becket was up to his old tricks again. When Henry asked for advice, one bishop said, 'My lord, while Thomas lives, you will not have peace and quiet, nor see good days'.

3

4 As Henry heard this he flew into one of his famous rages. He was once seen rolling on the ground in his palace chewing the rushes which covered the floor. Waving his arms around, he called out, 'Are you all cowards? Will no one rid me of this troublesome priest?' Four knights heard this.

The knights were the king's servants. They wanted to show their loyalty to Henry. Without speaking to him, they sailed across the Channel to England and rode at top speed to Canterbury.

After a while Henry calmed down. When he heard that the knights had gone, he guessed what they were going to do. He sent messengers to stop them. But it was too late. The knights were soon at the cathedral and were searching for the archbishop.

STEP 2

Go through the story again very carefully. Copy out the table below. Fill the first column with as many facts from the story as you can. Fill the second column with the parts that still puzzle you.

New facts which help to explain the murder	Parts of the story I still don't understand
Becket and the king had been quarrelling before.	Why did Becket ask the Pope to punish the Archbishop of York?

Years before the murder

You still have a lot of questions. To answer them you will need to go even further back in time! The final part of the story shows you that trouble had been brewing for many years.

When Henry became king in 1154 he chose Becket as his chief adviser. They became good friends. They worked hard to make the country strong. Henry and Becket were a good team. Together, they stopped wicked barons from running unfair courts.

Murder? That's very naughty

Sorry

The Church courts which tried monks and priests were also unfair. They were not as harsh as the king's courts. Some priests even got away with murder!

In 1161 Henry asked Becket to be the new Archbishop of Canterbury. He hoped that Becket would control the Church courts. When Becket finally accepted, in 1162, Henry got a big shock! Becket had changed! He had started to serve a new master – God. He sometimes spent whole nights praying. Henry was amazed.

Henry still hoped that Becket would help him to end the power of the Church courts. But Becket refused. Then he upset Henry by expelling a baron from the Church without asking the king's permission. Henry made him promise never to do this again.

Henry now passed a law saying that all serious Church court cases had to be tried again in the king's courts. Becket gave in at first but then, in 1164, he changed his mind. King Henry was furious. Becket guessed that he was in danger and ran away to France.

In 1170 Henry tried to show that he did not need Becket. He ordered the Archbishop of York to crown his son as the next King of England. This job was supposed to be done by the Archbishop of Canterbury. Becket was furious. How dare Henry use the wrong archbishop!

When you started this enquiry, all you knew was that a group of angry knights killed an archbishop. Now you know that a much bigger quarrel lay behind it all. The knights had very little to do with it, but they somehow got caught up in a big problem.

Think

- How did Becket's actions make the quarrel worse?
- How did the king's actions make the quarrel worse?

STEP 3

At the time, everyone would have blamed everyone else.
Match up each of the speech bubbles with one of the four people.

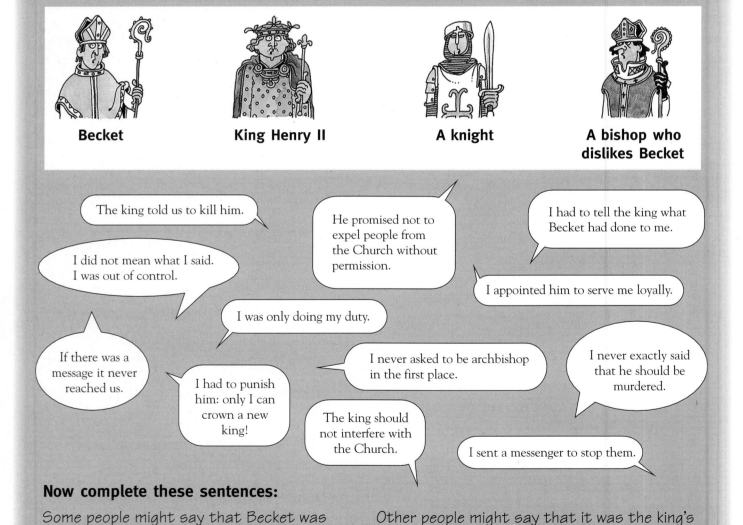

Becket   **King Henry II**   **A knight**   **A bishop who dislikes Becket**

The king told us to kill him.

He promised not to expel people from the Church without permission.

I had to tell the king what Becket had done to me.

I did not mean what I said. I was out of control.

I appointed him to serve me loyally.

I was only doing my duty.

If there was a message it never reached us.

I never asked to be archbishop in the first place.

I never exactly said that he should be murdered.

I had to punish him: only I can crown a new king!

The king should not interfere with the Church.

I sent a messenger to stop them.

Now complete these sentences:

Some people might say that Becket was responsible for his own death because ...

Other people might say that it was the king's fault. The king made the problem worse by ...

More than a murder mystery

But none of this tells you very much. In some ways it does not really matter whose fault it was. What matters is what the story tells you about medieval times.

The knights were caught up in **something bigger**. Henry and Becket were also caught up in **something bigger**. The murder did not happen simply because Becket was determined and stubborn. It did not happen simply because Henry II had a bad temper. Henry and Becket were caught up in a big problem faced by all medieval kings. This picture shows the problem.

It's my job to show that I'm in charge of EVERYBODY in the country, INCLUDING priests and bishops!!

It's my job to make sure that the government does not take any power from the Church.

Most medieval kings thought like this

Most medieval archbishops thought like this

Perhaps the clash was worse in Henry's reign because of Henry's and Becket's personalities. However, deep down, the problem was that **it was very difficult for any medieval king to control the Church.**

Thinking your enquiry through

So why was it so difficult for kings to control the Church? You are going to write an essay. The introduction and the start of all the other paragraphs have been written for you. Choose details from the story to help you to complete each paragraph.

Your introduction

There were lots of reasons why it was difficult for medieval kings to control the Church. The story of Thomas Becket shows just how difficult it was.

Your second paragraph

The Church was determined to keep control of its own special courts. For example, Becket refused...

Your third paragraph

Very important churchmen, such as Becket, already had lots of power. For example...

Your fourth paragraph

Very important churchmen sometimes wanted even more power! For example...

Your fifth paragraph

Medieval kings wanted to stay in charge of everyone in the country, including the bishops. For example...

Your conclusion

Overall, I think that things came to a head during the reign of Henry II because...

Challenging the crown
Could the rich control the king?

This modern statue stands outside the Houses of Parliament in London. It shows Richard I, who ruled England from 1189 to 1199. Around the picture you can read some of the qualities which medieval people expected their king to have.

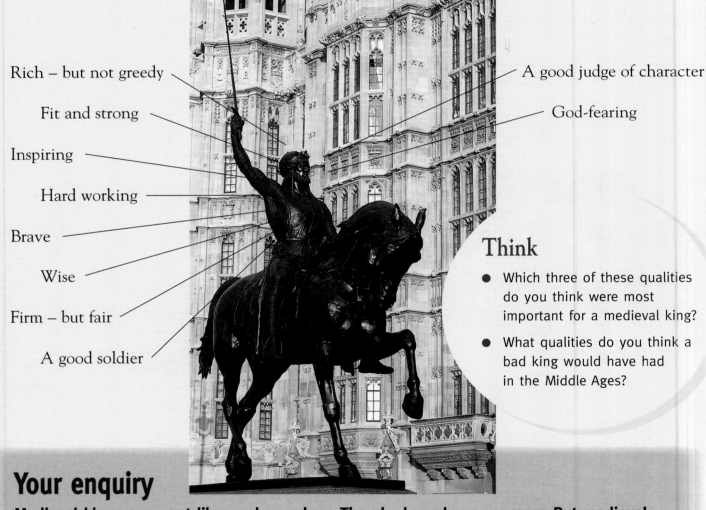

Rich – but not greedy

Fit and strong

Inspiring

Hard working

Brave

Wise

Firm – but fair

A good soldier

A good judge of character

God-fearing

Think

- Which three of these qualities do you think were most important for a medieval king?

- What qualities do you think a bad king would have had in the Middle Ages?

Your enquiry

Medieval kings were not like modern rulers. They had much more power. But medieval kings could get into serious trouble if they did not have the qualities shown in the picture. In the thirteenth century some barons forced two unpopular kings to give up some power ... and that was only the beginning. In this enquiry you will find out how the richest people in the country began to challenge the king. **You will see how surprised medieval kings would be at the way the country is run now.**

Magna Carta

King John manages to upset everyone

The first king to give up some of his power was John. He is famous as Prince John in the make-believe stories of Robin Hood. In the stories he is a wicked and foolish prince who taxes the people of England unfairly. Some historians say John was just as foolish in real life. Others say he was simply unlucky.

John ruled England from 1199 until 1216. He faced the following problems.

Problem number 1

He quarrelled with the Pope about how to run the Church. From 1208 until 1213, the Pope banned all church services in England and English people feared that they would all go to hell. Some Church leaders blamed John for the trouble.

Problem number 2

John went to war twice against the French king. His army was badly beaten both times. He lost almost all the land that his father had gained in France.

Problem number 3

John raised taxes in England to pay for the wars. This upset his barons. He ordered them to pay far more tax than earlier kings had done.

Prince John from Walt Disney's Robin Hood

Think

- For how many years did the ban on church services last?

- Why do you think the barons gave John the nicknames Softsword and Lackland?

- Which of the three problems do you think upset the barons most?

The barons strike back

In 1214 many barons rebelled against John. They believed that he could not rule the country properly and was treating them unfairly. If someone did not do something the whole country would be ruined! In 1215 they forced John to grant a charter. This charter described the liberties or rights of **freemen** in England. This did not mean everybody, of course. Millions of peasants were villeins, not freemen. The charter said what English kings could or could not do to freemen. This was the first time anyone had expected an English king to obey a set of rules. The charter later became known by the Latin name **Magna Carta** which means 'great charter'.

Here is a photograph of Magna Carta. Some of the main points in it are given in modern English.

The king must not interfere with the Church.

When a baron inherits land he should pay the king no more than £100.

The king cannot collect new taxes unless the barons and bishops agree.

No freeman can be put in prison without a proper trial with a jury.

The king's men must not take anyone's goods without paying for them.

Justice will be given without delays or bribes.

Traders must be able to travel freely without having to pay tolls.

Think

- Use the examples from Magna Carta to work out the different ways in which John had been upsetting people.

- What was so new about Magna Carta for English kings?

- At the time, Magna Carta was not designed to help everybody. What kind of people were not helped by the charter?

Unexpected results from Magna Carta

John did not keep the promises he made in Magna Carta. He was fighting the barons again when he died in 1216. The new king, Henry III, was only nine years old. He had a wise adviser called William Marshal who changed Magna Carta slightly and told the barons that Henry III would accept it. Every king or queen since then has also had to accept it – with a few changes of course. It controlled their power for hundreds of years.

In those centuries more and more people became freemen. This meant that ordinary people had their rights protected, not just the wealthy barons, knights and bishops. This was not what the barons had expected. It was not what the barons wanted. They wanted rights for freemen, but not for everyone. When people start something new they cannot be sure where it will lead.

STEP 1

Make a list of ways in which John upset the barons. Sort your ideas under these headings:

Church

Money

Justice

Make sure you remember to use all the points from Magna Carta listed on page 68.

The first Parliaments

Henry III and the Great Councils

Henry III was King John's son. He ruled from 1216 to 1272. The early years of his reign were quite successful – but that was when William Marshal and others were helping him. When he was old enough to rule without help he began to make some serious mistakes. Here are two of them.

Mistake number 1

Henry upset most English barons by inviting many French friends and relatives to advise him. The English barons felt that they were being ignored.

Mistake number 2

Henry was a very religious man. He always seemed to do whatever the Pope wanted. He allowed the Pope to raise huge sums of money from people in England.

The barons and Church leaders saw that their own power was slipping away. In 1258 they forced Henry to call a Great Council. A Great Council was a meeting in which the king asked his leading barons and bishops for advice. All kings held one from time to time.

Henry III at the Great Council. A fifteenth-century picture

At the Great Council in 1258 the barons did not give Henry advice: they gave him orders! They threatened to go to war with him if he did not hand over his power to a group of fifteen barons and bishops. The leader of this group was Simon de Montfort.

Henry gave in to the barons for a while but dared to fight them in 1264. Simon de Montfort crushed the king's army and became like a king for a year. He was the most powerful man in England.

Think

● What was a Great Council?

● Why was the Great Council of 1258 different from earlier ones?

New people in the Great Council

The other barons soon turned against Simon de Montfort. They thought that he had too much power. Simon knew he was losing their support so he called a new type of Great Council of his own. He invited only barons and bishops who he knew were on his side. But he still needed more support. So he also invited knights from every county and rich men called **burgesses** from towns that were friendly to him.

This was the first time that people from the towns had ever been asked to give support and advice at a Great Council. The towns were growing richer. Without them the country would have been poor and weak. Rich merchants said it was only fair that they should have some say in what happened. All Simon knew was that he wanted the support of as many rich people as he could find.

Parliament comes to stay

In 1265 Simon de Montfort was killed in a battle. It was King Henry's son, Prince Edward, who defeated Simon's forces at the Battle of Evesham. It looked as if the king would be in control again, but the idea of inviting rich men from the towns to the Great Councils did not die with Simon.

Prince Edward later became King Edward I. When he needed money to pay for a war, he copied Simon's idea. By this time the Great Council had become known as **Parliament**. The word 'Parliament' comes from the French word *parler* which means 'to talk'.

Hmm... their support may not be enough.

I know! I'll get support from the richest men in the towns and shires too!

In 1295 Edward called a Parliament made up of himself (the **monarch**), the **Lords** (barons and bishops) and the **Commons** (knights and burgesses).

This Parliament became known as the Model Parliament. It has been the pattern or model for Parliaments ever since.

Parliament in 1295

Edward was still enormously powerful but from his time onwards, kings discussed taxes with people who were not even nobles. In the fourteenth century kings needed money so badly that they even made deals with Parliament. The people had begun to control the king.

Think

- Knights and burgesses were rich and important, but not as important as the bishops and barons. What do you think the bishops and barons thought about all these new people in Parliament?

- Once the king had started to include knights and burgesses in Parliament, why do you think it would have been very difficult to stop them coming?

STEP 2

Write three sentences about the ways in which Parliament was beginning to challenge the king's power. Hunt for information about these three points.

Bossy barons and bishops.

New people from the towns and the counties.

The king's need for money.

Parliament today

Parliament still has three parts: the monarch, the Lords and the **Commons**. It still does the same sort of work: deciding on taxes, making laws and discussing difficult problems. The leaders still need some of the skills which kings needed in the Middle Ages but much has changed. The Commons have most power and the monarch has least power. The Lords have a small amount of power.

The picture on the right shows what Parliament is like today.

The members of the Commons are called Members of Parliament or MPs. They are voted into power at elections.

Every adult can vote for an MP.

Neither the voters nor the MPs have to be rich any more.

Both men and women can vote or can be MPs themselves.

Voters get the chance to choose new MPs every five years or so at a General Election.

The person who has most power now is the Prime Minister. He or she is an MP. The Prime Minister suggests new laws or taxes and asks the Commons to agree. They discuss the plan and take a vote. If most MPs agree with the plan it will become law.

Parliament today

The Lords discuss the plan as well and can make a few changes to it. However, the Lords cannot stop the Commons getting what they want. The Commons are in charge. The monarch has to agree to any plans that the Commons and the Lords want. Richard I would never believe it!

Think

- Which is the most powerful part of Parliament now?

- What do you think King John would say about Parliament today if he knew this?

- Look again on page 66 at the qualities which medieval kings needed. Which of these qualities would a modern Prime Minister not need?

Use the diagrams and the section called 'Parliament today' to find examples to put under the following headings:

<u>Parliament today is similar to Parliament in 1295</u>

<u>Parliament today is different from Parliament in 1295</u>

Thinking your enquiry through

Imagine that King John has come back to life. He wants to know what has happened to the way in which England is governed.

You must break the news to him. You must explain what has happened since the twelfth century. The first paragraph has been started for you. You must finish it. Use all the information that you noted down in the Steps. Take care. He might be very angry!

I'm terribly sorry Your Majesty, but I'm afraid things got a lot worse after you died. First of all, your son Henry made an even bigger mess of things than you did. He upset the barons so much that they ...

Peasants in revolt

9

How did the peasants get out of control?

It was all over. They had failed. The peasants looked up at the rotting bodies of their friends hanging by chains and ropes from the trees. They wondered why they had let themselves be tricked. It had all changed in those few moments outside the city walls of London. They could have taken the life of the boy king. They could have cut him down in a shower of arrows from their bows. But their leader had gone and they just did not know what to do. They had dared to trust their king. They had travelled back to their villages in their thousands. But the young king had lied. They were not made free. His soldiers had killed their friends. Their revolt had achieved nothing.

Your enquiry

The words opposite sound like part of a story. They are. They tell what happened in 1381 when the peasants got out of control. In this enquiry you are going to tell the whole story of the Peasants' Revolt. Your story will have three parts. These will be called:

Part 1 Trends and triggers
Part 2 Threats and violence
Part 3 Death and defeat.

You must not simply make up the story. Historians have to work out what really happened. This is often a challenge, but it is good fun as well.

Trends and triggers

Before you can write the first part of your story, you must understand why the peasants became rebels and rose up against their king.

Some things had been making the peasants angry over many years. We call these things trends. Other things sparked off the revolt in 1381. We call these things triggers.

These peasants will explain what went wrong and why they started a revolt.

The priests are telling us that we are just as good as the lords. One poor priest, John Ball, has been put in prison for spreading this idea.

England has been at war with France for nearly 50 years. Since 1369 the war has been going badly. It is costing a lot of money. I have heard a rumour that the French might invade.

When Richard II came to the throne in 1377 he was only a boy of ten. His advisers are useless. They do nothing to help us.

Since the Black Death in 1348 wages have been going up. In 1351 there was a new law which said that no peasant could ever be paid more than he was before the Black Death.

The king's commissioners have been sent to the villages to make sure we all pay the new taxes.

Since the Black Death in 1348 some of us have been able to buy our freedom from the lords. But many peasants are still villeins. They are not free.

These new **poll taxes** – 1377, 1379 and now 1381 – will ruin us! Every person over 15 has to pay 4d. How can we afford it?

Your first challenge is to sort out the causes into trends and triggers. Good historians never mix up their ideas! Make a chart like this and decide where to put the information.

Trends	Triggers
Some peasants were becoming free, but many were still villeins.	There was a new poll tax in 1381.

Now you can write the first paragraph of your story. First of all, explain why the peasants were becoming angry. Use the information under the Trends heading in your chart. Then, using the information under the Triggers heading in your chart, write about what sparked off the revolt.

Threats and violence

In the last week of May 1381 the peasants' anger finally burst into violence. There were serious problems in many places in England but the worst trouble happened in the south east. The map will help you to understand the story.

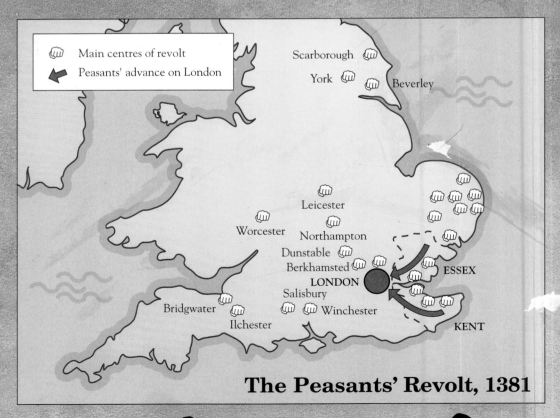

Key:
- Main centres of revolt
- Peasants' advance on London

The Peasants' Revolt, 1381

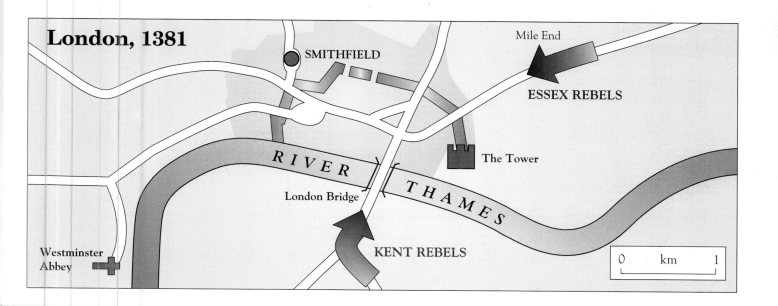

London, 1381

Mile End

SMITHFIELD

ESSEX REBELS

RIVER THAMES

The Tower

London Bridge

KENT REBELS

Westminster Abbey

0   km   1

In May 1381 some villagers in Essex attacked a poll tax collector. A judge was sent to punish the villagers, but he was forced to return to London. Three of the judge's clerks were beheaded. Their heads were put on poles and paraded around nearby villages. Soon after, peasants started to attack the local lords. They burned manor houses and murdered their owners.

A few days later villagers in Kent copied them. Some peasants even attacked the monks in local **abbeys**. Before long the countryside was out of control. The leader of the Kent rebels was Wat Tyler. Tyler and his men took over the king's castle at Rochester and marched into Canterbury.

Thousands of peasants then marched towards London. Only the king could solve their problems.

On Thursday, 13 June, some poor Londoners helped the **commons** to get through the gates of the city. The rebels smashed and burned the houses of the king's advisers.

Sudbury, the Archbishop of Canterbury, and Hales, the king's Treasurer, hid themselves with the king in the Tower of London. That night the 14-year-old king, Richard II, watched from the high windows of the Tower. Below him, thousands of drunken rebels went through London burning houses and murdering lawyers and foreign traders.

On Friday, 14 June, Richard met the rebels at Mile End. He promised them that all peasants would be free from that day and he told them to go home. Many did. But others wanted more. They blamed the king's advisers for their problems and wanted blood. They broke into the Tower of London, dragged Sudbury and Hales outside, and cut off their heads. It took eight blows to remove Sudbury's head. The peasants fixed his hat on his head with a nail and put it, with others, high above London Bridge for all to see. It was a sign that they were deadly serious. They refused to return home until their leader had met Richard once more.

The second part of your story is going to be tricky to write. There is too much information here. You cannot include everything. Your second challenge is to pick out the key points that show who the peasants' anger and violence were aimed at. Make a list of these. This might be your first one:

May 1381, Essex peasants attacked poll tax collector.

Now use your list to write the second part of your story.

Death and defeat

Thousands of peasants were still in London. King Richard agreed to meet them just outside the city walls on Saturday, 15 June. But everything changed when their leader, Wat Tyler, was killed. The king repeated his promise to set them free. They trusted him and went home. As you know, he broke his promise, their leaders were hanged and no one gained freedom. The Peasants' Revolt had failed.

The picture on this page shows the death of Wat Tyler, but the artist was not there at the time. No one knows for certain how he was killed. Historians get most of their information about the Peasants' Revolt from **chronicles**. The chronicles were books written shortly after the revolt. Most were written by monks who did not see what happened. They just wrote down what they heard from other people. Each one tells the story slightly differently as you will see. A historian may have to use all of them to decide what happened. It is rather like a jigsaw – but not all the pieces fit!

KING RICHARD in great danger in the CITY of LONDON and the REBELS discomfited.

The death of Wat Tyler

Chronicle 1

Wat Tyler approached the king at Smithfield on a little horse. He dismounted, holding a dagger, and shook the king roughly by the hand. He swore, with a great oath, that he would not leave until the king granted their wishes. The king said Wat could have all he wanted and ordered him to go home.

Tyler sent for a jug of water and rinsed his mouth in a rude manner in front of the king before climbing on his horse again. One of the king's men called out that Tyler was the greatest robber in Kent. Wat wanted to strike the man with his dagger, but the mayor stopped him.

Wat stabbed the mayor but he was wearing armour and was not harmed. The mayor drew his own dagger and cut Wat deeply in the neck and with a great blow on his head. Another of the king's men ran his sword through Wat's body two or three times. Wat rode towards the commons and then fell to the ground half-dead.

Wat was carried to a hospital. The mayor went there. He told some men to carry Tyler back to Smithfield and to cut off his head.

Chronicle 2

On Saturday at the Plain Field the king met Walter, the tiler, who was the rebels' leader. This man did not show respect to his majesty. He spoke strong words to the king with his head still covered and with a threatening look on his face.

The mayor tried to arrest the tiler who drew his knife and tried to stab him. The mayor wounded him with his sword and another man grabbed his head and threw him off his horse. The whole mob of countrymen cried out, 'Our chief is killed!'

Chronicle 3

The king arrived at Smithfield. He was approached by Walter the tiler who failed to uncover his head. The mayor said to him, 'Why are you speaking to the king in that way? Take off your cap.' Tyler replied, 'You are a traitor!' A royal servant immediately stabbed Tyler with a dagger. Then the mayor and another man did the same. And so the tiler died.

Chronicle 4

At Smithfield the king was approached by the rebels' leader. His proper name was Wat Tyler but he is now known by a different name, Jack Straw. Tyler drew close to the king. He threw his knife from hand to hand like a boy playing a game.

Jack Straw spoke threateningly to the king and grabbed the bridle of his horse. When the mayor saw this, he feared the king might be killed. He knocked Jack Straw into the gutter with his sword. Another man pierced his side with his sword. So he fell on his back and died while his hands and feet quivered for some time.

The last part of your story is going to be the trickiest to write. You need to work out from the chronicles how the peasants' leader, Wat Tyler, was killed.

Use a table like this to collect information from the four different Chronicles.

	Chronicle 1	Chronicle 2	Chronicle 3	Chronicle 4
What Wat Tyler did				
What the mayor did				
What the king's man did				

Thinking your enquiry through

Now it's time to finish your story of the Peasants' Revolt by explaining how Wat Tyler was killed. Work out from your table all the facts that the chronicles agree about.

In your last paragraph you should explain:

- where the peasants met the king
- what Wat Tyler did
- what the mayor did
- what the king's man did
- what happened after Wat Tyler was killed.

Challenging England 🔟

Why did people support Owain Glyn Dŵr?

These are the ruins of a castle in a high and lonely place in south-west Wales. It is Carreg Cennan. Look at the countryside around it. Think how difficult it would have been to attack this castle.

In 1403 Carreg Cennen was attacked and captured by Welsh forces. The Welsh were rebelling against the English. They were led by **Owain Glyn Dŵr. Owain Glyn Dŵr wanted Wales to be free.**

Your enquiry

For over a hundred years, the Welsh had not dared to challenge the English in this way. Now, they were mounting a bigger challenge than ever. Owain Glyn Dŵr did not just want Wales to be free. He was planning to conquer England too! What made the Welsh people support such bold plans? Why did the revolt of Owain Glyn Dŵr gain so much support?

Owain Glyn Dŵr: a great leader

Long, long ago, before anyone alive in 1403 could remember, King Edward I of England had fought wars with Wales. After a long struggle, Edward brought Wales under English control. In 1301 Edward I even made his own son the 'Prince of Wales'. England had controlled Wales through her towns and castles ever since.

Now, a hundred years later, Owain Glyn Dŵr was saying that **he** was Prince of Wales! He announced it in 1399. In some ways, this was nothing new. Others before him had claimed to be descended from the Welsh princes of long ago. The poets had written of the glories of the Welsh past. They dreamed of a future when the princes would rise again.

But Owain Glyn Dŵr began to **behave** like a prince. He was crowned. He set up his court at Harlech Castle. He called Welsh parliaments. He started to govern parts of Wales as a monarch would.

The rebellion did not succeed. It fizzled out by 1408. But for a long time the English were very concerned. Owain Glyn Dŵr was confident of success. In 1403 he had much support. Things looked promising for the Welsh.

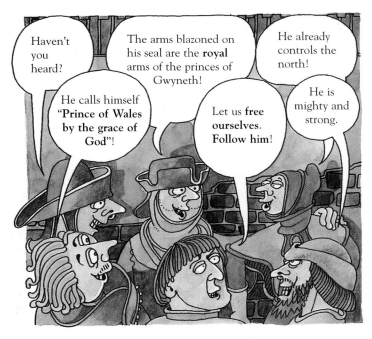

Owain Glyn Dŵr's promises and plans were not just empty words. By the time Welsh forces were in the region of Carreg Cennan castle, he had gained control of many key places in Wales. Find Carreg Cennan on the map below.

As news of Owain Glyn Dŵr's successes spread, there was panic amongst the English officials and settlers in many towns. The forces of Owain Glyn Dŵr were advancing quickly.

In the small town of Kidwelly, the constable was in total despair. He wrote to the King:

All the rebels of South Wales, helped by the men of France and Brittany, are advancing on the castle with all their power. They have destroyed all the corn in the countryside around the castle. Many of the townsmen of Kidwelly have fled to England with their wives and children; the rest have retreated into the castle and are in great fear for their lives.

Think

● Why were the English of Kidwelly in danger?

● What else does this letter tell us about the power of the rebels?

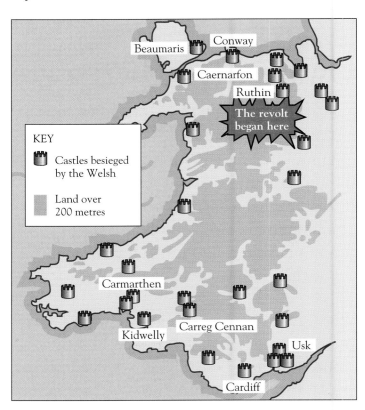

Wales at the time of Glyn Dŵr's revolt

STEP 1

Copy down the three statements below. Look again at all the stories, pictures and evidence in this enquiry so far. Find examples to match each statement.

Owain Glyn Dŵr was a skilful military commander.

Owain Glyn Dŵr was feared by the English.

Owain Glyn Dŵr inspired the Welsh people and gave them hope.

Big friends and big plans

Far away, up in the north of England lived the powerful Percy family. The earls of Northumberland always came from the Percy family. Here are three things which you need to know about the **Earl** of Northumberland:

1 He was ambitious.
2 He had **very** big plans.
3 He wanted to be more powerful than the king of England!

So, the Earl of Northumberland decided to support Owain Glyn Dŵr.

In 1405, a meeting was held between three important people:

1 Owain Glyn Dŵr, the Welsh leader.
2 The Earl of Northumberland.
3 Edmund Mortimer. Mortimer was another powerful English lord who believed that his family should be the rulers of England.

These three people decided that they would defeat the English king and then divide England up between them.

Owain Glyn Dŵr had other supporters in Ireland and Scotland too. He knew that there were people in those lands who had had enough of English control. He also decided to make friends with the French.

Making friends with the French was a very clever thing to do. England had been fighting France, on and off, for a very long time, in the Hundred Years War. Owain Glyn Dŵr's rebellion happened right in the middle of it.

The alliance with the French was not empty words either. It actually happened. In August 1405 a fleet of 140 French ships landed on the coast of Wales at Milford Haven. In the ships was an army of 2,600 French troops.

STEP 2

Look back over the last section. Copy the statements below. Then find information which supports each statement.

Owain Glyn Dŵr was taken seriously by other countries.

Owain Glyn Dŵr was taken seriously by important English nobles.

Owain Glyn Dŵr took **himself** very seriously.

Support from the Welsh

The inspiring words of a great leader can be very important. However, people do not rise up in rebellion just because a great leader comes along! Usually, there is a great, big, tangled knot of reasons why people support a person like Owain Glyn Dŵr. And usually, somewhere in that tangle, **money** matters are involved.

Here are some facts about Wales in the late fourteenth century, just before Owain Glyn Dŵr's revolt.

Fact One – Powerful towns

By the fourteenth century there were about 90 towns in Wales. These towns were very small, but very important. Important townsmen (or **burgesses**) held law courts, made rules and had all sorts of trading privileges just as in English towns.

Many burgesses were extremely rich. They owned a lot of land in the countryside around the town. They often controlled all the trading activity in the area around the town. The burgesses of Carmarthen controlled all the trade within a 15-mile radius.

But wasn't that true of most English towns too?

Fact Two – Powerful townspeople (Welsh ... and English!)

Welsh towns were not exactly like English towns. Some of the important townspeople were Welsh. Others were English. In some parts of Wales the towns were more English than in others. Sometimes where the Welsh townspeople were very rich the English townspeople were very jealous. This happened more and more in the later fourteenth century. In some towns the English tried to strengthen their control by reviving old laws against the Welsh (or by making new ones). In 1393 a new statement was included in the town charter of St Clears:

> No burgess must be judged by any Welshman... but only by English burgesses and true Englishmen.

Fact Three –
Difficult times for towns

Taxes were high all over England and Wales. English kings needed a lot of money for all those wars. This was bad enough, but it came at a time when the Black Death had made life very hard. Earlier in the century, lots of people died from the Black Death. This made trading difficult. Sometimes when times are hard people get more competitive. They try to protect their own privileges and keep others out.

These three facts on their own do not tell us very much, but if you put them together, they start to tell us a lot. You must try to work out how they are connected.

1a Write down one sentence summing up each of the three facts above. Draw boxes around your facts.
b Now draw arrows between your three boxes to show how each of these facts could affect the other facts and make problems worse.

Now you should understand why some Welsh people were getting more and more angry about English rule towards the end of the fourteenth century.

Thinking your enquiry through

The rebellion of Owain Glyn Dŵr failed. It is still a very important part of British history however. It tells us a lot about how different people thought and what different people wanted.

Make your own copy of this map. Finish each of the statements with as many ideas as you can. To help you, read the enquiry again, and look at the notes which you made for your Steps.

The Welsh people supported Owain Glyn Dŵr because…

The English noblemen supported Owain Glyn Dŵr because…

The French King supported Owain Glyn Dŵr because…

The crown and the sword

Which kings had most control?

This picture shows an idea that was popular in the Middle Ages. It is the Wheel of Fortune. In the centre of the wheel is a woman. She represents Fortune which is rather like luck. On the right you can see a king who is out of luck and is falling. The person on the left is rising. He hopes to be king.

The Wheel of Fortune

Some medieval kings had good fortune. They were strong and successful. Others were not so lucky. Look through this table about medieval kings. You will find some curious details!

Medieval kings. A chronicle of death and war

King	Reign	How the king died	Wars
William I	1066–87	Died after being injured in battle	Conquered England
William II	1087–1100	Killed by an arrow while hunting – possibly murdered	Won wars against Scotland, Wales and his brother
Henry I	1100–1135	Serious indigestion – after eating too many eels	Won a war against his brother
Stephen	1135–54	Heart attack	Won a long civil war against his cousin
Henry II	1154–89	Fever	Won land in Ireland and France. Lost war against wife and sons
Richard I	1189–99	Killed in war	Successful in Crusades and in wars against France
John	1199–1216	Dysentery (fever with serious diarrhoea)	Lost civil war
Henry III	1216–72	Old age	Wars against France. Lost a civil war against barons, then won another
Edward I	1272–1307	Old age	Won wars against Welsh and Scots
Edward II	1307–27	Murdered – possibly with a red-hot poker	Lost wars against Scots and French. Lost civil war against his wife
Edward III	1327–77	Old age	Won wars against France
Richard II	1377–99	Probably murdered	Lost wars in France. Lost civil war
Henry IV	1399–1413	Severe skin disease	Won civil war. Won wars against Scots, Welsh and French
Henry V	1413–22	Dysentery	Won wars and land in France
Henry VI	1422–71	Murdered	Lost war in France. Lost throne in civil war (The Wars of the Roses)
Edward IV	1461–83	Severe indigestion	Won the throne, and lost it for a while, in civil war (The Wars of the Roses)
Edward V	1483	Disappeared – probably murdered	No war, but forced off the throne by uncle (The Wars of the Roses)
Richard III	1483–85	Killed in battle	Won war against Scots. Lost civil war (The Wars of the Roses)

Think

- Which kings were murdered or died in battle?
- Which kings fought civil wars against barons or members of their own family?
- Which kings fought wars against the Irish, Welsh, Scots or French?
- Which kings belong on the left of the Wheel of Fortune? Which kings belong on the right?

Your enquiry

Some medieval kings found it a lot harder to control their kingdoms than others. In this enquiry you will decide which English kings (there was only one queen) had most control over their kingdom and which had least control. On the following pages six English rulers explain what happened during their reigns.

Mother and son – Matilda and Henry II
Queen Matilda 1141 to 1154

Queen Matilda

“ How dare they leave me off that list of English rulers! I was a true Queen of England – even if I was never properly crowned. My father, Henry I, left the throne to me. He made all his English barons swear that they would accept me as their queen. Some kept their word and served me faithfully. But others sided with the so-called King Stephen, my foul cousin, who had dared to steal the throne from me.

My armies fought for years against Stephen. But his barons were powerful. They built massive castles without asking permission. The whole country was out of control. War dragged on. I captured Stephen in 1141 and ruled alone. The following year, Stephen escaped and our civil war continued as fiercely as ever. In the end I gave up my claim to rule. Stephen promised that when he died my son Henry could become king. ”

King Henry II: 1154 to 1189

" What a mess this country was in when I took over from King Stephen! I worked non-stop to put things right. I hardly ever sat down, even at meal times. There was too much to do.

I had to sort out the barons for a start. I wasn't going to have them rising up against me or using their soldiers to rob my people. I tore down over 300 of their castles. I sent judges around the country to give people fair trials. With my friend Thomas Becket I sorted out the whole system of law and order.

I ruled far more than England of course. I conquered Ireland. I took over huge areas of France. I won some of France by war. Other parts belonged to my wife Eleanor. You can see my huge **empire** on this map.

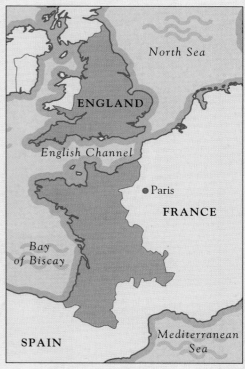

The empire of Henry II

I controlled the greatest empire in Europe. But I could not control my family or my closest friend Becket. Becket refused to bring the Church under my control. It cost him his life! My wife and sons turned against me. Within 25 years of my death my sons had let my empire crumble away. **"**

Henry II shown in a stained-glass window in Winchester Great Hall

STEP 1

Make a chart like this one. Put in as much information as you can about Matilda and Henry II.

	In control	Out of control
Matilda	She won the throne for a while in 1141.	Many barons fought against her.
Henry II		

Father and son – Edward I and Edward II

Edward I: 1272 to 1307

Edward I shown in a stained-glass window in Winchester Great Hall

"" My father Henry III was a good man but a weak king. He ignored his barons. I didn't make that mistake. I kept them involved. In fact I went further. I called knights from the counties and rich **burgesses** from the towns to my Parliament. I kept them happy so they would pay all the taxes I needed for my wars.

It's strange that my nickname was The Hammer of the Scots. After all I never really controlled the Scots. But I certainly beat the Welsh! Their chief, Llewellyn, and his brother David refused to accept me as their lord. In 1282 I finally forced my way into their mountain stronghold. Within a few months both were dead.

Wales was mine. I built five massive new castles. No one had ever seen anything so fine. After that, the Welsh never really broke free of English control.

I am sure I could have taken full control of Scotland as well. I had already hanged their leader William Wallace in 1305. Their new king Robert Bruce would have fallen at my hands too. But I was old. I died as I led my army north. It was up to my son, Edward II, to finish the job. ""

Edward II: 1307 to 1327

The tomb effigy of Edward II from Gloucester Cathedral

"My father wanted me to conquer Scotland, but I knew I could never be a soldier like him. He left orders that our army should carry his bones into battle against the Scots. What nonsense! I turned the army around and returned to London. Years later, in 1314, I did fight the Scots. It was a disaster. They crushed us at the Battle of Bannockburn in 1314. I gave in. The Scots had won the right to have their own kings.

I was not really interested in taking new lands. I preferred to spend my time swimming, rowing or cutting hedges. The barons hated me for not being like my father. They hated my companions and advisers as well. They even murdered my closest friend.

The weather was against me too! We had terrible harvests and animal diseases for many years while I was king. My people said God was punishing me for my faults.

It was my wife who ended my reign. Isabella – or the She-wolf as we called her – had left me and gone to France. In 1326 she invaded England, butchered my chief adviser and forced me to give the throne to our son. I was taken away and killed.
I will spare you the awful details. All I will say is that people miles away from the castle heard my screams – but not a mark was found on my body."

STEP 2

Add more information to your chart. Put in as many points as you can about Edward I and Edward II.

Another father and son – Henry V and Henry VI

Henry V: 1413 to 1422

" When I became king I knew what my country needed. It needed strong leadership and the glory of war. I did very little in England. I longed to win back all those lands in France that England had owned in past centuries. Besides, if I kept the barons busy in war against the French they would not be able to rise up against me.

I invaded France in 1415. It was a good time to attack. The French king had gone mad and his country was weak. At first all went well but then disease struck my army. Thousands died. I decided to return to England. Before we could reach our ships a massive French army trapped us near a village called Agincourt. The army was four times as big as our English force – but we still beat them.

The Battle of Agincourt opened the way for other victories. By 1420 the French king promised that I would take his throne when he died. I was going to be King of England and France. It never happened. There are some things we cannot control. In 1422 I was struck down by a foul disease and died at the age of 35. **"**

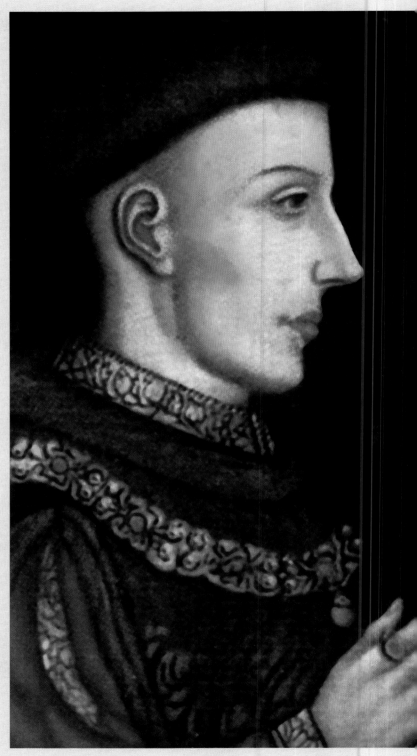

Henry V

94

Henry VI: 1422 to 1471

"My father was Henry V. When he died, I became King of England at the age of nine months. When the French king died, I became King of France as well. I was the only person in history to rule both these great kingdoms.

A sixteenth-century picture of Henry VI

That sounds very impressive. In fact I had little real control. In the first 15 years of my reign everything was done for me by advisers. That suited me. I did not like power and war. I was more interested in books and paintings. Above all, I loved God. I spent my time and money setting up new schools, colleges and churches. While the barons quarrelled over who should have power, the French took back almost all their lands from us.

For a while in 1453–4 I went mad. This started 30 years of civil war. My wife and the barons struggled over who was the true king. I lost the throne to a baron who called himself Edward IV. My supporters won the throne back for a year but I hardly cared. In 1471 Edward took over again and had me murdered. It must have been God's will."

STEP 3

Finish your chart by adding all the points you can about Henry V and Henry VI.

Thinking your enquiry through

Draw an outline of the Wheel of Fortune at the beginning of the enquiry.

1 On the left, next to the man who is rising, write about three monarchs who had good control. Explain why you chose them.

2 On the right, write about three monarchs who had poor control. Explain why you chose them.

The power and the glory

Why could no one ignore the Church?

Here is a story and a picture from a twelfth-century book about King Edward the Confessor.

A poor cripple called Michael went to see the Pope in Rome. The Pope was the leader of the whole Church. He told Michael that God would heal him if the King of England carried him into Westminster Abbey. Michael travelled to England and told the king what the Pope had said. The king lifted Michael on to his back. Blood began to flow from the crippled man's sores on to the king's clothes. But the king kept on. He carried Michael all the way to the altar of the abbey. As he did this, Michael began to feel his legs begin to stretch out. When the king put him down, Michael was able to stand alone. Soon he and the king were running and jumping and singing God's praise!

Your enquiry

Nowadays we find it hard to believe stories like this. Many people now ignore the Church. Even people who go to church probably do not expect to see miracles like the one in the story. The Church may not matter much to many people now, but you could not ignore it if you lived in the Middle Ages. In this enquiry you will find out why it was so important. When you gather information it helps if you sort it out under different headings. You will use these three: Power, Hope and Help. At the end of the enquiry you will make a board game to show why no one could ignore the Church.

The Church had power

The word 'church' can just mean a building but it can also mean the organisation to which all Christians belong. By the Middle Ages nearly everyone in Europe belonged to it. It became known as the Catholic Church. The word catholic means 'all-including'.

This diagram shows some of the main people who ran the Church. Ordinary people were very unlikely to see the Pope, bishops or archbishops. But they often saw their parish priest.

At the head was the Pope.

Below him were arch-bishops and bishops.

At the bottom were the parish priests.

He was very powerful. He was God's representative on Earth.

They were rich and powerful. They owned a lot of land and advised kings.

They were often very poor. Most of them worked very hard.

The parish priest had the power to forgive people's sins if they told him what they had done wrong. If people kept on sinning, the priest had the power to report them to the Church courts. These courts punished bad behaviour in different ways.

Think

- What different types of punishment did the Church use?

- Why do you think that the Church punished people for sins like these?

- Church records show that these punishments were not used very often. Does this prove that the power of the Church made most people behave themselves?

97

Another important job for the priest was collecting money from the villagers. Some had to pay rent to the Church because it owned their land and their house. Everyone had to pay a church tax which was called the **tithe**. Each year the parish priest collected one-tenth of the new-born animals and one-tenth of that year's crops. The money from these goods went to the bishop. This made the Church very rich. Bishops controlled rents and jobs for thousands of peasants who lived on Church lands. Bishops became like barons!

STEP 1

1   See if you have understood why the Church had so much power over people. Match up these Heads and Tails to make sensible sentences.

Heads

The Church had power over people because the Pope...

The Church had power over people because bishops...

The Church had power over people because parish priests...

Tails

...collected tithes from villagers.

...was seen as God's representative on Earth.

...were like barons and advised kings.

2   Make up some more sentences which explain why the Church had power over people.

3   For the board game you will need three sets of cards: Power Cards, Hope Cards and Help Cards. Use the sentences you made above to write your Power Cards. A Power Card might say:

<u>Power Card</u>

You have not paid your tithes. Move back three spaces!

Make as many cards as you can.

The Church gave people hope

But if the Church was so horrible to people, why did they put up with it?

This picture shows what happened to sinners who went to hell. The Church did not just control people's land, money and behaviour. It tried to control their beliefs as well. It taught that life went on even after the body had died. Without the help of the Church a person's soul would go to hell. In hell it would suffer agony forever. Pictures like this were seen in churches. Priests used them to show what happened to souls in hell.

Hell was obviously a place of awful suffering and pain. If people only heard about hell they would have very little hope indeed.

In fact the Church did give hope. It said that most people's souls did not go straight to heaven or hell. Instead, the soul went to a place called **purgatory**. It would stay there until all its sins had been burned away. When the soul was free of sin it went to heaven. It would live there forever in joy and glory.

Think

● What is happening to these people in hell?

● Why do you think the Church made hell seem so frightening?

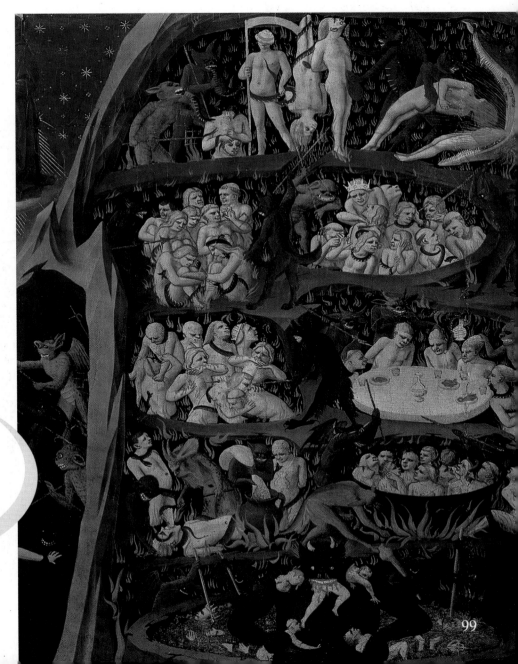

Sinners in Hell.
A fourteenth-century picture

99

Purgatory was not as bad as hell, but it was still painful, and a soul might spend hundreds of years there. If you wanted your soul to move more quickly from purgatory to heaven, the Church had plenty of ideas. Here are some of the Church's suggestions for giving people hope.

1. 'Trust in the power of your priest'

Everyone had to join the priest at the service of **Mass** each Sunday. The Church said that the priest's prayers at Mass turned bread and wine into the body and blood of Jesus. When people confessed their sins to the priest he would use his special power to grant forgiveness. The priest had to baptise every new-born child or it would go to hell if it died.

A Latin mass attended by four laymen, 1400

2. 'Use saints and relics to help you pray'

People believed that God would be kind to them if they asked for help from the saints or the Virgin Mary. Some churches had **relics** to help people pray. Relics were objects connected with a holy person. A relic might be the bones of a saint, some of his dried blood, his big toe – or even his head. Relics were sometimes kept in boxes like this.

A reliquary which contained the relics of St. Thomas, 1190

John Lydgate and the Canterbury Pilgrims. A fifteenth-century picture

3. 'Go on a pilgrimage'

Some people stopped work for a while and travelled on pilgrimages. This was a kind of special journey for God. They went to churches that held relics or to places where a miracle had happened. Some **pilgrims** went thousands of miles to Jerusalem where Jesus had died. One of the most famous books of the Middle Ages was about a group of pilgrims. It was called *The Canterbury Tales* and was written by Geoffrey Chaucer.

4 'Trust monks, nuns and friars to pray for you'

Some men and women served God and helped His people by becoming **monks** or **nuns**. They lived in a monastery or a nunnery. They prayed for people's souls. In the later Middle Ages monks called friars travelled around the country telling people about Jesus. **Friars** were very poor.

Nuns praying

5 'Buy a special pardon'

Men called pardoners travelled around the country. They carried relics or written documents from the Pope. If someone touched these and gave some money to the Church, it was believed that they would spend less time in purgatory.

The Pardoner from 'The Canterbury Tales', 1400–1410

6 'Build a chantry chapel'

Rich people such as merchants or nobles used their money to add **chantry** chapels to churches. Priests chanted prayers in them so that the dead person's soul spent less time suffering in purgatory.

Greenway Chantry Chapel,
St Peter's Church, Tiverton, Devon

7 'Live a good life'

There were seven really good deeds which helped a person to go to heaven quickly. These were:

1 giving food & drink to the hungry
2 clothing the naked
3 warning people about sins
4 visiting prisoners
5 caring for the sick
6 giving shelter to the homeless
7 burying the dead.

STEP 2

Now make the Hope Cards for your board game. Here are two examples of a Hope Card.

Hope Card
You have confessed your sins to a priest.
Move forward two spaces.

Hope Card
You are very rich. You have built a chantry where your soul will be prayed for.
Move forward six spaces.

The Church gave people help

Most medieval people had a hard life. If the harvest failed they would go hungry or starve. Disease was all around them. Very few had the chance of an education. So what could the Church do to help?

Simply going into a church might help people by cheering them up. The church would be the best building in most villages. It would be strong, dry and safe. Churches were full of life and glowed with colour in the Middle Ages. The walls inside were covered with paintings of saints. There were colourful statues and carvings. The sun would shine through stained-glass windows to show pictures from Bible stories. See how colourful and lively this church is.

The church and the churchyard were used for all sorts of events. Weddings often happened in the porch or churchyard so that everyone knew that a couple had been married. Other events at the church included feasts, fairs, puppet shows, archery contests and dances. There were also drinking parties known as church ales and mystery plays. Events like these cheered people up. The whole village could meet, share news and gossip.

Think

- Which of the events described here would still happen at a church?
- Which of the events above would happen in a community centre or village hall nowadays?

The church building even helped to give people a sense of time. The priest would ring the bell regularly. This gave some idea what time it was.

The Church also arranged holy days when people did not have to work. Our word 'holidays' comes from this. These holy days and Sundays were the only days off work for most people.

Cullompton Church, Devon

The best priests, monks and nuns cared for others around them. They had a duty to help the sick, the old and the poor. They also helped travellers who needed shelter. They used money from tithes to pay for this care. Some **monasteries** grew all sorts of herbs and plants to make medicine.

If the priest could read and write he might have taught some Latin to a few villagers. Only people who knew Latin would have got on in the world. Most poor families would not have had time for this. Children from richer families might have been taught by monks in monasteries or cathedrals. Some boys might have gone to a university run by the Church.

The Church encouraged rich people to help the poor. Money used in this way was called **alms**. Some built almshouses for old people to live in. Others rebuilt their local church. To modern minds this seems a strange thing to do. But medieval minds were different from ours. Perhaps people rebuilt churches to impress God. Perhaps they did it to make their town seem greater than others.

Whatever the reason, the buildings are still standing as a sign of how important the church was to people in the Middle Ages.

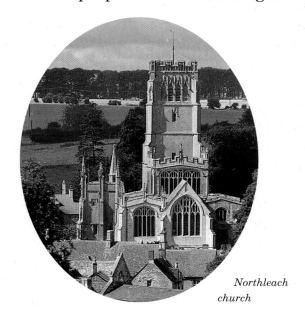

Northleach church

STEP 3

Make your Help Cards. The first one could say, 'A monk has found herbs to heal your daughter. Go forward two spaces'.

Make as many as you can.

Thinking your enquiry through

So why was it impossible to ignore the Church in the Middle Ages? Your board game should show how much you have understood.

You will need to make a board with clearly marked squares. Some squares should tell a player to pick up a Power Card or a Hope Card or a Help Card.

You could decorate the board with pictures from this chapter. You could have other special squares too.

Remember! Your board game will be a good one if it helps the players to learn more about why no one could ignore the Church.

God's grumblers
Why risk death to change the Church?

The burning of Sir John Oldcastle, 1417

This picture shows something which happened in 1417 in England.

Think

- What is happening to the man in the centre of the picture?

- Suggest some reasons why this might be happening to him.

- What do the other people seem to think about it?

Historians often need extra information to help them make sense of pictures. This short story will tell you more.

In 1413 the Archbishop of Canterbury sent some men to arrest Sir John Oldcastle. The archbishop said that Oldcastle had been spreading false beliefs about God and lies about the Church. This was called **heresy** – and the punishment was death by burning.

Sir John escaped and led a short rebellion against the king with some friends who shared his beliefs.

They called themselves **Lollards**. They believed that the Catholic Church had gone terribly wrong and that most English people were not true believers.

In 1417 Sir John was recaptured. He was put on trial and burned at the Tower of London. The archbishop was happy. The Church carried on as before.

Your enquiry

Sir John Oldcastle knew that it was very dangerous to criticise the Church. So why did he do it? Why did changing the Church matter so much? Why was it better to burn to death than to let the Church go on as before? In this enquiry you are going to find out more about the Lollards. You will then be able to work out for yourself why the Lollards risked death to speak out against the Church.

The man behind the Lollards

The name Lollard comes from an old word meaning 'a person who mumbles or grumbles'. The Lollards were grumbling about the Church. They said it did not follow the true teachings of Christianity.

This is the man who started these attacks on the Church. He was called John Wycliffe.

A woodcut of John Wycliffe

Wycliffe lived from 1320 until 1384. He was a priest who taught at Oxford University. Wycliffe studied the Bible carefully and thought about what it said. He had three main complaints.

Complaint number 1

The Church is too rich and powerful.
It ought to give away its money.

Complaint number 2

The Church allows wickedness.
It ought to show how to live a good life.

Complaint number 3

The Church encourages **superstition**.
It ought to teach what the Bible says.

Wycliffe knew that it was dangerous to make these complaints but powerful friends protected him. By the time he died he had translated the Bible from Latin into English. He had thousands of followers. Most of them were quite poor. They wanted the Church to change its teaching and to give away its fortune.

Think

- Why do you think that Wycliffe translated the Bible into English?

- Why do you think that the Church wanted the Bible to stay in Latin?

The king and the Archbishop of Canterbury thought it was bad for people to criticise the Church. In 1401 they passed laws which said that anyone who spread Wycliffe's heresy or used a copy of his Bible would be burned alive. That was why Sir John Oldcastle was burned to death in 1417. In 1429 Wycliffe's bones were dug up, burned to ashes and thrown into a river.

But Wycliffe's ideas lived on. Groups of Lollards risked their lives by reading the English Bible to people. After 1500 Wycliffe's ideas helped to change the Church forever.

STEP 1

At the end of this unit you will do a role play. One person will pretend to be a cloth weaver who knew Wycliffe and agreed with his ideas. He or she will have to explain who Wycliffe was and what his main ideas were. Here are some questions to help you prepare for your role play.

1 Which of the words below will the cloth weaver use to describe Wycliffe and his feelings about the Church? happy, sad, angry, clever, brave, weak, sincere, greedy

2 Write down five important facts about Wycliffe which the cloth weaver must try to use in the role play. You should include Wycliffe's complaints about the Church.

Now you must find out more about Wycliffe's three main complaints. On the next three pages are some examples of the way he attacked the Church. They are written as if he is preaching a sermon. This sermon is made up, but it has been put together using different sources from the Middle Ages.

The Church is too rich and powerful

"My Brothers and Sisters in Christ, our dear Lord Jesus must be deeply hurt by the riches and power of the Pope. Pope John had 25 million gold crowns when he died! Why should the Pope be such a great lord if Christ Himself did not even have a house? Now we have two men claiming to be the true Pope. They are raising armies to fight against each other. They serve the Devil not God.

In our own land many bishops ignore the Church. They spend their time advising kings or squeezing money from Church lands. I know a bishop who has only been to his cathedral once!

Remember Bishop Stapledon of Exeter? He made himself a fortune before he was murdered by the mob in London. He served his master the king by raising taxes – but he filled his own pockets as well. He made a generous gift to his cathedral, **but does God want His house to be built with money taken from the poor?**

Many monks and friars are no better. Years ago the friars were poor, honest preachers. But now, most live together in grand houses. They pay for these by begging and by pleasing the rich with easy promises of God's forgiveness.

We see the rich trying to buy their way into heaven. Merchants and nobles buy pardons from the Pope himself. They build chantry chapels where priests pray for their souls.

But God is not fooled.
He rewards simple faith."

STEP 2

Now make some notes to guide another person in the role play. This person will be a baker. He has joined the Lollards because he thinks the Church is corrupt. In other words, it is too rich and powerful.

1 Which of the words below will the baker use to describe the Church and priests? *corrupt, generous, simple, greedy, powerful, helpful, shameful*

2 Write down five examples of how rich and powerful the Church is. The baker must try to include these in the role play.

The Church encourages superstition

" How are people to learn about Christ if the Church does not teach them? When they come to the service of Mass all they hear is Latin. It means **nothing** to them! **Nothing!** Many poor priests just learn the words by heart without knowing what they mean. Hardly any priests have their own Bible. Some try to teach what is right and what is wrong. But many give people the idea that the Church has some sort of magic which will take them to heaven!

Of course, people must attend Mass. But it is their faith which helps them, not the bread and wine alone. There is no magical power in the bread and wine or in the holy water which the priest uses to baptise children. But the Church tells people that they will not go blind on any day when they see the bread being blessed at Mass.

It tells the priest to drink any spider that falls into the wine because it has been washed in the blood of Jesus.

Priests take holy water and sprinkle it on the fields to help crops grow. Some villagers scrape up wax from church candles. They melt the wax on to the dung of their enemy, believing that his backside will rot away. Is this what Christ wants us to learn?

My good people, we all know that relics help us to pray, but why does the Church suggest that relics have magical powers? We have fingers, arms or teeth from countless saints. Churches claim to have bottles containing Christ's breath or his tears. Sick pilgrims think these relics will heal them. My brothers and sisters, **this is not faith**. It is magic. But how can our people learn the truth if the Church will not let us study the Bible in English. We must hear God's holy words. "

STEP 3

Now make some notes to guide another person in the role play. This person will be a Lollard priest. He has joined the Lollards because he thinks the Church does not teach the truth about God.

1   Which of these words will he use to describe the beliefs of most people? sensible, foolish, wicked, confused, pure, sincere, superstitious, mistaken

2   Write down five examples of how people thought the Church had magical powers to help them. The Lollard priest must try to use these in the role play.

The Church encourages wickedness

"Finally, dear friends, I ask you to think about the way many so-called Christians live. Some priests are drunk when they lead church services. Others sell holy bread or water. Monks and nuns are put in the stocks for bad behaviour. One of our bishops went all the way to France to steal a relic. He chewed a piece off the arm of the Virgin Mary. Worst of all, hundreds of churchmen have been tried for murder in our special Church courts and are let off lightly.

The people behave as badly as their priests. Some fight in church. They push to the front at Mass so that they can get out quickly afterwards. Friars get drunk and dance with women on holy day feasts. The women arrive late to church so that everyone will notice them in their fine new dresses. Men swear and gamble with dice. And have you heard the clowns entertaining pilgrims with dirty jokes as they line up to see relics?

Some people even break our rule of **sanctuary**. You all know that a criminal cannot be arrested in the church grounds. But more than one person has simply walked into a churchyard and killed an enemy who was hiding there. These murderers then walk straight into the church to ask for forgiveness!"

Monks behaving badly

Now make some notes to guide another person in the role play.
This person will be the baker's wife. She has joined the Lollards
because she thinks the Church is letting wickedness grow.

1   Which of the words below will she use
    to describe people's behaviour?
    good, bad, sinful, harmless, funny, kind,
    unforgivable, evil, serious, wicked

2   Write down five examples of bad
    behaviour which show that people are
    not living as true Christians. The
    baker's wife will try to talk about all
    these in the role play.

Thinking your enquiry through

Work in groups. Each group must have
enough people to play these parts:

  * the cloth weaver (a Lollard)
  * the baker (a Lollard)
  * the priest (a Lollard)
  * the baker's wife (a Lollard)
  * a market trader.

The group is meeting in secret. Remember
that you will be burnt alive if you are
discovered. The Lollards are trying to
persuade the market trader to join them.

1   Prepare carefully.
    a   The four Lollards should start by
        comparing the notes which were
        made in Steps 1 to 4. Decide what
        each of you will say to persuade
        the market trader to join you.
        Check that your notes are as full as
        possible. Help each other to get all
        the key points.

    b   The market trader should make a
        list of reasons why he might not
        want to join the Lollards. You could
        look at the work you prepared for
        Enquiry 12 for more ideas.
        Remember how strict and
        frightening the Church could be!
        Alternatively, your teacher might
        like to be the market trader.

2   When you are thoroughly prepared, you
    can role play your conversation. Take it
    in turns to speak.

3   When everyone has finished speaking
    the market trader should decide
    whether to join the Lollards or not. The
    market trader must give plenty of good
    reasons for his decision. They must not
    be modern reasons. They must be the
    sorts of reasons which medieval people
    would give.

The most important place on earth for Christians was Jerusalem in Palestine. Jesus had died there. Christians wanted to go there on pilgrimage. They wanted to see holy relics like the crown of thorns worn by Jesus and the nails from the holy cross. But Palestine was not part of Christendom. Even though Christians called Palestine their **Holy Land** they did not control it.

The Holy Land was ruled by Muslims who followed a different religion called Islam. Jerusalem was a holy city for Muslims as well. For hundreds of years they let Christians go on pilgrimages to Jerusalem and all was well.

Think carefully about the information you have looked at so far. Use it to begin making a list of reasons or motives for going on a crusade. You could start your list like this:

Motives of Crusaders
Jerusalem was the most important place in the world for Christians.

As you work through the enquiry you will be adding more motives to your list.

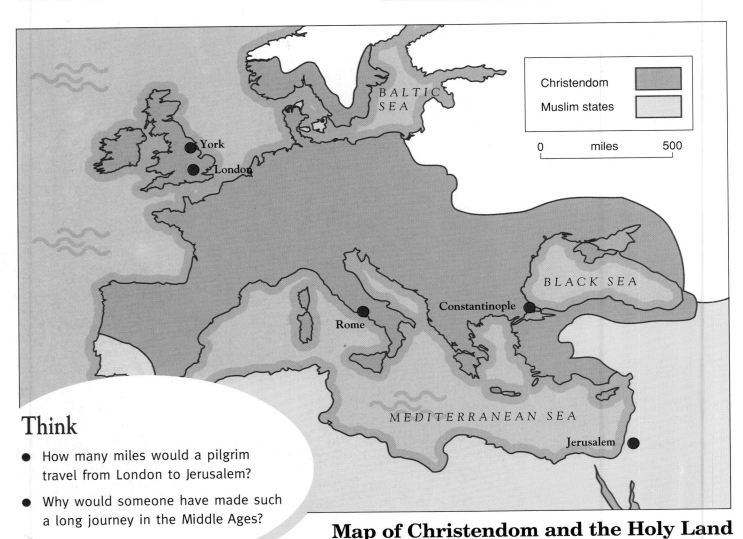

Think

- How many miles would a pilgrim travel from London to Jerusalem?
- Why would someone have made such a long journey in the Middle Ages?

Map of Christendom and the Holy Land

The Crusades begin

In 1071 a different group of Muslims took over Palestine. These were the Turks. They stopped pilgrimages and attacked Christian lands in the east of Europe. The Pope promised to help the Christians in the east. In 1095 he preached a sermon which called on all Christians to win back the Holy Land from the Muslims or Saracens as they were often called. This is what the Pope said:

> **❝** Brothers, I speak as a messenger from God. Your fellow Christians in the east desperately need help. The Saracens have attacked them and have pushed deep into Christian land. They are killing great numbers of Christians. They are destroying churches and land. In the name of God, I beg you all to drive out these foul creatures.
>
> Your own land has too many people. There is not much wealth here. The soil hardly grows enough to support you. Set out for Jerusalem. Take that land from the wicked infidel and make it your own.
>
> If you die on the journey or if you are killed in a battle against these Saracens all your sins will be forgiven at once. God Himself has given me the power to tell you this.
>
> Some of you have spent too much time fighting against your fellow Christians. But now you must fight the Saracens. Let bandits become soldiers. Soldiers who have been fighting for money must now fight for heavenly riches. **❞**

Pope Urban II's sermon, 1295

Think

- Find three places where the Pope suggested that God told him what to say.

- Why do you think the Pope suggested that his message came from God?

- The Pope called the Saracens 'foul creatures'. How had they upset him?

- The Pope wanted to make joining a crusade sound attractive. How did he do this?

STEP 2

You should be able to add some more motives to the list you started in Step 1. Here are some words to help you:

Obeying God

Revenge

Land

Forgiveness

Love of war

The crusader knights

During the two hundred years from 1095 to 1291 thousands of Christians did what the Pope wanted. All sorts of people went on crusades. Monks and nuns and soldiers' wives all joined in. There was even a Children's Crusade in 1212. It was led by a 12-year-old shepherd boy. But the most famous crusaders were the knights.

Knights trained very hard to be fierce soldiers. They practised in **tournaments** and tried to impress the women who watched.

a

A knight loves to prepare for war in tournaments. He sees his own blood flow and feels his own teeth crack when his opponent hits him. He is thrown to the ground and rises again twenty times. Then he is ready for war.

By a twelfth-century English writer

b

Alas, my darling! It breaks my heart to leave you, but I must go to the Holy Land. That is where I will win paradise and praise and your true love.

A letter from a French crusader to his wife in 1190

A fourteenth-century painting of knights fighting on horseback at a tournament

Think

- What was a tournament?
- How did medieval knights try to impress women?

Each crusader had to kneel and make his promise to God. He said he would try to capture Jerusalem from the Saracens and visit the place where Christ had been buried. After making this promise the crusader had the sign of the cross sewn on to his clothes.

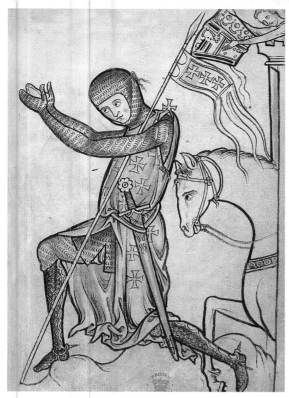

Picture of a Crusader knight from an English chronicle, thirteenth century

The Crusades were like most wars in the Middle Ages. They were full of brutal and horrible killing. Prisoners were sometimes sawn in half, buried alive or used for target practice. The heads of captives were fired from slings back into their own camp.

A thirteenth-century picture of Crusaders and Saracens fighting

Think

● Why is this knight kneeling?

● How can you prove that the knight in this picture is a crusader?

● Why do you think the woman on the right is giving him a helmet?

c

Ten thousand Saracens suddenly attacked us. They threw javelins and shot arrows, yelling horribly with wild voices. They are terrifying soldiers. Some of our men felt like running away but the bravest remembered that it would be an honour to die for Christ and fought back harder than ever.

An account of a battle in the Third Crusade, written by an English priest in the late 12th century

d

The day after the battle his friends went searching for his body. Finally they found him. His face was so thick with blood that they hardly recognised him. They wrapped the body and carried it back to the town. The king came to his funeral. Prayers were said for the knight's soul. Nobles laid the body in its grave with tears in their eyes.

An account of a crusader knight's funeral, written by an English priest in the late 12th century

STEP 3

Use the information in the section called 'The crusader knights' to add some more motives to your list. Here are some words to help you:

Honour   Bravery   Love

Other crusaders

There were nine crusades between 1095 and 1291. Thousands of knights from all over Europe were killed in the Holy Land. They gave their lives to God and served him by prayer and by war. But some crusaders had other reasons for going.

1

> Many have gone on crusades to escape from their own land. There are criminals, thieves, robbers, pirates, dice-players, men who have left their wives and women who have left their husbands.

By a French priest, thirteenth century

2

> My dear wife, I now have twice as much silver, gold and other riches as I had when I set off on this crusade.

From a letter written by a French crusader to his wife, 1098

3

> You have been found guilty of hitting a priest on the head with your sword. For this outrage you must join a crusade or pay a suitable soldier to go instead.

From an English trial, 1291

4

> People heard that the Pope would grant a pardon to all who went on a crusade. That is the only reason they went.

By a French writer, 1204

Between the wars there were long times of peace when Christians and Muslims became friends, traded and shared ideas. People in Europe gained a lot from Muslims as the diagram below shows.

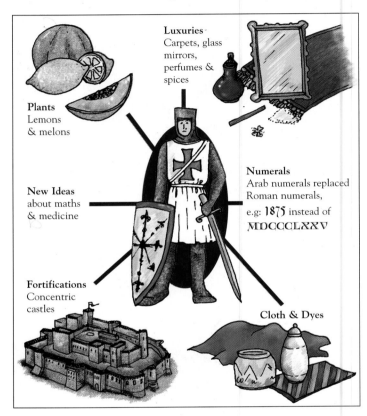

Plants
Lemons & melons

Luxuries
Carpets, glass mirrors, perfumes & spices

New Ideas
about maths & medicine

Numerals
Arab numerals replaced Roman numerals, e.g: 1875 instead of MDCCCLXXV

Fortifications
Concentric castles

Cloth & Dyes

Think

- Why might some people join the crusaders in the Holy Land even when there was no fighting taking place?

STEP 4

Now finish your list by adding more motives from the section called 'Other Crusaders'.

Thinking your enquiry through

So why did medieval people risk their lives by joining the Crusades? You are now going to write an essay to answer this question. You have made a long list of motives. At the moment your ideas are in no particular order. You need to sort out the motives and organise them so that your essay will be clear.

1 Sort out your list by arranging the motives under these headings. Choose better headings of your own if you prefer.

Controlling Jerusalem

Getting to heaven

Bravery, love and honour

Other reasons

2 Each group of motives will form one paragraph in your essay. Start your paragraphs like this, or use your own ideas if you prefer.

The crusaders wanted to control Jerusalem. This was important because...

Crusaders thought that they would be sure of a place in heaven. We know this because...

Bravery, love and honour were very important to crusader knights.

Some people had other reasons for going to the Holy Land.

3 Remember that historians always have to support what they say with facts. You will need to look back at the different sections in this enquiry to find details which support your ideas. You could even use small quotations to make your essay stronger. Do it like this:

One example of knights going on a crusade for love is in a letter from a French crusader to his wife. He wrote, 'I will win paradise and praise and your true love.'

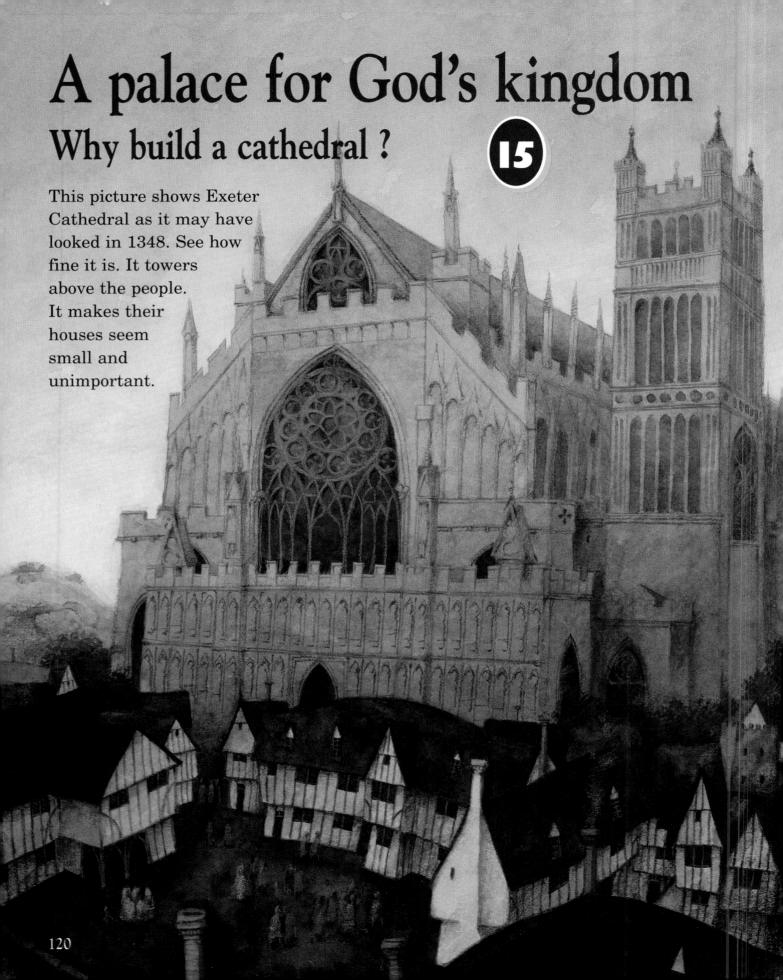

A palace for God's kingdom
Why build a cathedral ?

15

This picture shows Exeter
Cathedral as it may have
looked in 1348. See how
fine it is. It towers
above the people.
It makes their
houses seem
small and
unimportant.

Think

- What is the cathedral made from?

- Why do you think so many parts of the cathedral are pointing up to the sky?

Your enquiry

You are going to find out why people in the Middle Ages spent so much time and money building cathedrals. You will base your work on the story of Exeter Cathedral. First, you will guess what decisions the cathedral builders made. Then you will find out what really happened. By the end of the enquiry you will understand what medieval people thought about their cathedrals.

In 1257 Bishop Branscombe sat down with his **chapter** (advisers) for yet another meeting. They were discussing what to do about the city's Norman cathedral. In many ways they loved it – especially its two famous towers. But it was dark inside and in some ways it made Exeter seem old-fashioned.

The bishop reminded the chapter about the amazing new cathedral at Salisbury. It reached high into the sky with tall arches pointing up to heaven. Inside it was filled with beautiful light streaming through large stained-glass windows.

Why couldn't Exeter have a cathedral like this? The city was proud of itself. It was growing in size and in riches. The bishop and his chapter wanted a new cathedral to hold more people and to show what a fine city Exeter was. Above all, it would be a palace for God's kingdom.

If you were the Bishop of Exeter and his chapter, what decisions would you make next? Look at the decisions they had to make and guess what they did.

1 Which part of the cathedral will you rebuild first?

a The west end called the **nave** where the ordinary people stand?

b The east end called the **choir** where the priests lead the holy service of Mass?

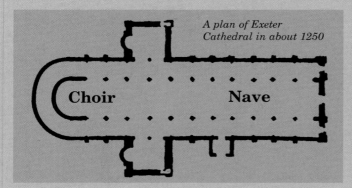

A plan of Exeter Cathedral in about 1250

Choir   Nave

2 How will you get the people of Exeter to support the changes?

a Remind them that a new cathedral will attract many pilgrims? This will be good for trade.

b Order them to do as they are told?

3 The work will cost a fortune. How will you raise the money?

a Ask people to give money now and in their wills when they die?

b Pay for the work yourselves?

c Sell pardons to people? These will get them into heaven quickly.

d Use all these methods?

4 You will need a mason to design the building and organise the work. Should he be:

a an expert who has already worked on many cathedrals – but he may cost a lot, or

b someone who has not worked on cathedrals before and who would cost less?

5 How quickly should the work be done?

a Finish in 20 years so people do not grow impatient?

b Take up to a hundred years – the cathedral is for God and He will wait?

6 You know that some stone masons carve picture-jokes in other cathedrals. Will you:

a let them carve jokes – after all, it is a place for ordinary people to enjoy, or

b stop them from carving jokes – it is God's house so everything must be serious?

You have made your own guesses about what happened in Exeter. Now read the story to see what actually happened.

122

The plans are made

The bishop and his chapter soon became excited by the idea. Priests led the Mass from the east end of the cathedral which was known as the choir. Christ himself was said to be there with them in the holy bread of the Mass. Surely it was their duty to make the choir more beautiful for Him? Many townspeople also wanted a fine new Lady Chapel for the Virgin Mary. Pilgrims would pour into Exeter to pray in the Lady Chapel and to see the cathedral's holy relics, which now included a strand of the Virgin's own hair! Pilgrims were good for trade too.

The building was for God, so only the best would do. They wanted top-quality builders and materials. Where would the money come from?

The bishop and chapter agreed to get things going. They promised to give large sums of money to help pay for the work. They were sure that local nobles and merchants would give money now or in their wills. One member of the chapter had a great idea: they could raise money by selling pardons to help people to get to heaven quickly.

After much prayer and discussion they were sure that God would provide all they needed. They decided to start by knocking down the east end of the cathedral and to replace it with a beautiful choir and Lady Chapel.

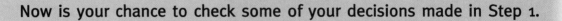

STEP 2

Now is your chance to check some of your decisions made in Step 1.

Make a table like the one below and fill in the second column with details from the pages you have read. Leave plenty of space between each point so that you can fill in more detail later.

Decision	What they did
1 Which part should be built first?	
2 How will you get the people of Exeter to support the changes?	
3 How will you raise the money?	

Which decisions did you get right? What were you wrong about?

The building begins

By 1270 the work was under way. The master mason was very experienced. He hired about 30 craftsmen and labourers. They knocked down the east end of the Norman cathedral. Barges and carts brought the finest timber and stone. The masons marked each stone with their own special mark. They knew they were paid for each piece they cut. The work was hard, and the work was dangerous.

A picture of medieval builders, thirteenth century

Year after year the work went on. Bishop Branscombe watched as the walls slowly grew, but he died in 1280, long before they were finished. So did the next bishop. Both men left money to keep God's work going. It was Bishop Bitton who saw the new choir and Lady Chapel finished. Shortly before he died in 1307, he gazed up in wonder at the beautiful high walls, the stained-glass windows and the bright colours of the vaulted roof pointing up to heaven. But if the people of Exeter thought their cathedral was finished forever,

they were very wrong.

Think

- What jobs are people doing in the picture?
- What does the picture tell you about the danger of the work?

STEP 3

Now check some more of your decisions by adding to your table:

Decision	What they did
4 Who should the mason be?	
5 How quickly should the work be done?	

The greatest challenge

The new bishop was a very powerful man. He was called Walter de Stapledon. He had worked for the Pope in Rome. He was very ambitious. He wanted to leave his mark on history.

The cathedral had been through forty years of building and fundraising. Money was short. Some people wanted to stop but the bishop wanted to carry on. He wanted to turn the inside of the cathedral into the shape of a cross. But the cathedral's famous towers were in the way! It seemed that nothing could be done. Some cathedrals in France had collapsed when builders went too far.

Bishop Stapledon refused to be beaten. He sent a challenge to Thomas of Whitney, the greatest master mason in England. Could he open up the space under the towers without letting them crash to the ground?

Between 1310 and 1320 God seemed to be at work through Stapledon and Whitney. They did the impossible. In those ten years the bishop and other priests gave about £1900 to pay for the work – nowadays that would be worth about £6 million!

Thomas of Whitney made huge, strong arches under the towers and a beautiful high ceiling between them.

Then, in 1326 came a terrible shock. **Bishop Stapledon was murdered!** In 1321 King Edward II had asked the bishop to be one of his advisers. Stapledon became one of the most powerful men in the country. He made a fortune. Just before he died he gave the cathedral a massive sum of money. He wanted to rebuild the whole west end completely. But he did not live to see this happen. He had made enemies. On 15 October, as he rode through the capital, a mob dragged him off his horse, cut off his head, stuck it on a pole and carried it through the streets.

STEP 4

Add some more details to your table. You should have found some extra information about raising the money, how long the building took and about the mason.

The work is finished

The new bishop was John de Grandisson. He carried out Bishop Stapledon's plans. A new master mason called William Joy was in charge and rebuilt the rest of the cathedral. The masons included comical carvings in the nave because this was the people's part of the cathedral. They left carvings of a pet dog, the cathedral cat and an acrobat who worshipped God by doing handstands!

Around the main door to the cathedral, the masons carved a marvellous scene of saints, kings, bishops and angels.

It was finished just in time. Soon after 1348 the Black Death reached Exeter. William Joy was one of thousands who died. But his work was finished. God's house was complete.

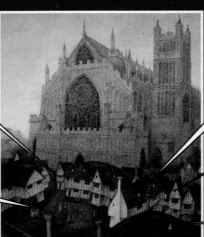

It will be good for our city to have a fine cathedral.

We built this for God, so we didn't mind spending a fortune on it!

God seemed to help us whenever we had problems with the building.

It just makes me think what heaven must be like.

It took us ages to build it.

STEP 5

1 **Add the last decision to your table and fill in the details.**

Decision	What they did
6 Should the masons carve picture jokes?	

2 **Answer these questions:**
a How many years had it taken to rebuild the cathedral?
b How many bishops were involved?
c How many master masons were involved?
d Why had it taken so long to rebuild the cathedral?

Thinking your enquiry through

So, what have you learned about why people built cathedrals? What has this shown us about medieval minds?

Copy the speech bubbles from the last picture. Under each one, write down some examples from the story of Exeter Cathedral which prove that people really did have ideas like these.

Glossary

abbey — Place where monks or nuns live and worship

abbot — Man in charge of an abbey

alms — Money given to help the poor

Anglo-Saxons — People who lived in England before the Normans arrived

apprentice — Young person who is learning a trade

archaeologist — Person who studies the past by digging up objects from the ground

archbishop — Very important Church leader

artefact — Object made by people

bailey — A large yard, part of a castle

barbican — A fortified gateway at the entrance to a castle

baron — Powerful nobleman

besiege — To surround a town or castle to force it to surrender

bishop — Important Church leader

burgess — Important person from a town

cathedral — Very large, important Church building

chantry — Place where priests pray for the souls of dead people

chapter — A group of people who advise a bishop on how to run a cathedral

charter — Document which gives someone certain rights

choir — The part of a church where priests lead the service

chronicle — Written account of events, often made by monks

clerk — Person whose job is to keep written records of events

commons — Ordinary people who are not knights or barons

conquer — To win control by war (A conqueror is the winner who takes control)

council — Group of people who share some power

crusade — A war which is fought to help the Christian religion

crusader — Someone who fights a crusade to help the Christian religion

earl — Powerful nobleman

empire — Group of countries ruled by one person

feudal system — The way in which people received land in return for some sort of work

freeman — Person who was free to move to look for work

friar — Monk who travels around

guild — Group of trades who made rules about their work

hall-keep — The inner part of a castle, where the lord lived

heresy — Beliefs which are not allowed by the Church

Holy Land — The area where Jesus lived and died

homage — A promise to serve someone

keep — The safest part of a castle

knight — Important soldier who serves a baron and the king

Lollards	Followers of John Wycliffe who grumbled about problems in the Church	**pilgrim**	Person who goes on a journey (pilgrimage) to a holy place
lord	An important person such as a baron or knight	**plague**	Serious disease which spreads quickly
manor	Area of land controlled by a knight	**poll tax**	Tax which has to be paid by every adult
mason	Person who makes stone buildings	**Pope**	The leader of the whole Roman Catholic Church
Mass	Important Catholic Church service	**portcullis**	A heavy gate which is dropped into place when a castle is under attack
medieval	Word which describes anything from the Middle Ages	**purgatory**	Catholics say that dead souls suffer here before being allowed into heaven
merchant	Trader		
military	To do with the army	**rebel**	Someone who fights (in a rebellion) against the person who rules over him
monarch	A king or queen		
monastery	Place where monks or nuns live and worship	**reconstruction**	Building or drawing made using evidence from the past
monk	A man who serves God by living and praying with other monks in a monastery	**relic**	Remains of a holy person or object, often used to help people pray
motte and bailey	A castle which has a large mound of earth (motte) and a large yard (bailey)	**sanctuary**	A custom which protected criminals while they were in the grounds of a church
nave	The part of a church building where the people stood	**siege**	An attempt to force a town or castle to surrender by surrounding it
nobleman	A powerful lord, such as a baron	**statute**	A law
nun	A woman who serves God by living and praying with other nuns in a nunnery	**superstition**	Belief in powers which seem almost magical
		tenant	A person who receives land or property in return for money or work
parchment	Animal skin used for writing or painting on		
Parliament	A meeting of the king's advisers to make laws or to discuss problems	**tithe**	Tax paid to the Church
		tournament	Sporting contest between armed knights
peasant	Poor farm worker	**villein**	A peasant who was not free to move away from his master's land
pedlar	Travelling trader		